French Canadian Roots

Researching Your French Canadian Family Tree and Genealogy

By Lawrence Compagna

The author has traced thousands of his direct ancestors, all the way into the middle ages, and arguably right back into antiquity. Using methods described in this book you can do the same, through your French Canadian ancestors, whose pedigrees are some of the best documented on the planet. The instructions are step-by-step, with tips on what to look for and how to progress rapidly. Your kin are waiting to be discovered and this book will help you find them.

Dedicated to my mother for encouraging me, Roseanne for opening the door, Madison for showing me how to be creative, Conrad for the intellectual stimulation, and finally to Wyatt ... who forever inspires me

French Canadian Roots

Fifth edition, copyright 2020

Edited by AMC

French Canadian Roots

Table of Contents

Note to reader:

As you go through this book, keep in mind that there is a glossary in the back. If any of the terms used confuse you, a definition or explanation may be available in the glossary that can clear things up.

Preface

"You're so lucky to have French Canadian ancestors," the librarian said. Her beige dress was long, and her light brown hair was arranged in a tight bun. I presumed that she was Mormon, since I was standing in the Family History Library in Salt Lake City, Utah... and this amazing collection of genealogical books was their doing. I had just finished asking her where they kept the books on Quebec, when she told me of her admiration for my long lost relatives.

"The French Canadians have some of the best family history records in the world... almost as good as Iceland," she mused as she escorted me to through the stacks of books. As she was talking, I looked at the volumes upon the shelves. We walked past books about New England, and I thought about how I should check these out later, because some of their family trees intersect with those of New France – the original name of Canada.

About one hundred feet further down, we came to a large collection of books on the French people of Canada.

"Most of the volumes deal with family history in the seventeenth and eighteenth centuries," the lady said.

"Makes sense," I mused. Most of the history seemed to deal with the period prior to 1759, the infamous day when France lost the Battle of the Plains of Abraham - and with it control of Canada to the English.

French Canadian Roots

Battle of the Plains of Abraham – General Wolfe's Death

After the battle, the large scale migration of French people to North America ended. As the Canadian Encyclopedia says "After New France was ceded to Great Britain in 1763, the migration of French colonists slowed considerably…Paris was not encouraging emigration to its former colony…from 1760 to 1850, only about 1,000 French people immigrated to Canada"

What this means is that if you are from Canada or the United States, and you have French ancestors, they most likely arrived in the New World prior to 1760.

"Thanks so much," I said to the lady as I began to look at the volumes on the shelves. As she turned to go back to the desk she had been sitting at, I thought of another question, "Is it true that there's a vault built deep inside of a mountain near here... filled with family history records?"

A soft smile flashed across her face, "Yes. It's true." She paused for a second, waiting to see if I had any other questions. Just before walking away, she smiled and repeated what she had said earlier, "You're lucky to have French Canadian ancestors."

*"**French Canadians** are an ethnic group who trace their ancestry to French colonists who settled in Canada from the 17th century"*

\- Wikipedia

Introduction

My name is Lawrence. I am an average guy.

I have a good job, three children, and my home is unspectacular. I like sports, reading, and going for long walks on the beach. *I am really, really average.* I even look average… except for my really nice glasses. They make me look really nerdy.

I have a passion for genealogy, but even that is unremarkable; I read somewhere that researching one's ancestors is one of the most popular pursuits on the internet.

What is not usual is what I have done with my genealogy hobby – I was able to trace thousands of my direct ancestors and push my line back beyond the middle ages, arguably right back into the time of the Romans.

Before I tell you about that, and provide some advice so that you can do the same, let me tell you how I got started.

How I Became Obsessed

One day, many years ago, my cousin was visiting my house. After describing her recent trip to Quebec, she unfolded a piece of paper and laid it down on the coffee table in front of me. I picked it up and looked at it. It was a chart... showing my namesake ancestors and their wives going back to the early seventeenth century. Each generation was listed, I think there were ten. At the top of the chart was my great, great - keep going for eight times or so - grandfather Mathias.

I was amazed. We knew our ancestors going back for four hundred years? I did not know it was possible.

This was back when the internet was still relatively young, the technology having been born a decade or so earlier. Its use in genealogy was still in its infancy as well, so most genealogical research was still done the hard way… in person… at an archive. This is what my cousin had done. She had a few scanned original documents to go along with the chart. One was particularly interesting - it was a ship's manifest from the year 1664. In that year, my ancestor Mathias came to the New World aboard a ship called the Black Holland.

Mathias was among the first Europeans in the Americas, and as I would realize later, it was for this reason that our descent from him was remembered… because he did something brave, adventurous, and spectacular - he was among the first Europeans to colonize an alien place they called the "New World".

After my cousin left, I became fascinated with the chart she left behind. However, it only listed this one branch of my family tree… was it possible to flesh out my entire line of descent? Even more intriguing, was it possible to push my ancestry even further back then Mathias?

My obsession for genealogy was born.

Assumptions

If you are reading this book, I assume a few things about you: One, you have French Canadian ancestors. Two, you may not speak French, or if you do, you are not fluent (however, if you do speak the language well, it will be a big plus when looking at original records). Third, you have a passion for genealogy. Fourth, you have a computer - this is important because you will uncover so many ancestors that you cannot keep up with just pen and paper. Fifth, you are adept at using a computer, or are willing to improve your skills in this area. Sixth, you are comfortable navigating the vast amount of genealogy resources that are now available on the web.

If this describes you, then you are in luck. I will help you uncover hundreds or even thousands of your direct ancestors, and - with just a little luck - even royal relatives. Together, we will push your family tree back to the middle ages, and you will uncover all sorts of interesting characters along the way.

"There was a long hard time when I kept far from me the remembrance of what I had thrown away when I was quite ignorant of its worth."

— Charles Dickens, Great Expectations

Great Expectations

In this book we will uncover your family tree, also known as your "pedigree". We will do this in a logical step-by-step manner, using tools that allow us to put together your tree as quickly and accurately as possible. But before we do this, we will examine the world of your illustrious ancestors who were the first Europeans to settle in the Americas, and look at their motivations for this move.

As you progress you will find people of note – the famous… and the infamous. Most of your ancestors will be farming folk, but a few will be writers, scientists, poets, warriors, heroines, victims, and especially explorers… because exploring and being a pioneer go hand-in-hand.

After we uncover your entire French Canadian family tree we will look at your relationship to living celebrities – people like Celine Dion, Angelina Jolie, Justin Trudeau, Justin Bieber, Madonna, and the Duchess of Cornwall.

We will then tackle a few more complicated topics, like the interrelationship of French and English history as it relates to genealogy.

At the end of this book, we will talk about travel to France and Quebec to understand the land and history better.

But first, let's talk about you and your relatives.

The Numbers

Expect to uncover every single member of every French Canadian branch in your family tree. You may have a gap or two for orphans, but you will find close to all of your long lost kin. The numbers in each generation will double, and in most cases you will go back about ten generations in each line before you hit a dead end –usually the parents of the pioneers are as far back as you can go. With ten generations of ancestors, your direct line will grow like this:

First generation: 2 (your parents)

Second generation: 4 (your grandparents)

Third generation: 8 (your great-grandparents)

Fourth generation: 16 (great-great grandparents)

Fifth generation: 32 (great x3 grandparents)

Sixth generation: 64 (great x4 grandparents)

French Canadian Roots

Seventh generation: 128 (great x5 grandparents)

Eighth generation: 256 (great x6 grandparents)

Ninth generation: 512 (great x7 grandparents)

Tenth generation: 1,024 (great x8 grandparents)

Conservatively, expect your tree to contain at least a thousand direct ancestors if it is entirely made up of French Canadians. Some of them will be members of the noble class, and their trees can be extended out for an additional twenty generations if they are members of an "ancient" family - one who traces their ancestry back to the middle ages. We will explore how to uncover this royalty and how to extend these lines further back in time.

Royalty

The Holy Roman Emperor - Charlemagne

You will find royal "gateway" relatives among your ancestors – those whose paths lead to kings, queens, dukes, princesses, barons, lords, and ladies. There were several nobles among the first French colonists, so chances are that you are going to encounter a small number in your family tree. The benefit of finding such people is that their pedigrees were already well established by the time they reached the New World, thus their trees can be pushed into the Middle Ages, and sometimes all the way back to the great Emperor Charlemagne who died in the year 814.

Charlemagne is considered the ancestor of all European royal families. After conquering almost all of Europe, the Pope crowned him "Holy Roman Emperor". His support of the arts and letters led to what is called the "Carolingian Renaissance", which dragged Europe out of the dark ages.

The reason that the pedigrees of nobles were so well documented, with an accuracy stretching all the way into the early Middle Ages, is that back in those days one's family tree was the basis for owning lands and titles - only nobles could own land, because the Kingdom of France operated under an inheritance concept called "primogeniture". Agnatic primogeniture meant that the eldest son inherits everything. If a couple had no sons, their title and land holdings went to the closest living male heir.

Henry IV, King of France 1589-1610

An extreme example of the concept of primogeniture is the true story of King Henry IV of France. Old Henry became heir apparent to the French throne in 1584 after the death of a distant cousin, because his well-documented family tree proved that he was the *most senior living direct male line descendant of King Louis IX ("Saint Louis) who had died over* **three hundred years earlier***.* Thus, Henry inherited the crown of France, and all of the lands owned by his predecessor. This example underscores how important family trees were among the French noble class, and how far back they stretched.

Explorers, Celebrities and Victims

You are likely to find explorers in your family tree, people like Jean Nicolet, the first white person west of the great lakes – and thus credited as the European who discovered Wisconsin.

Jean Nicolet – the first European west of the great lakes

A few of the other explorers you may come across are Etienne Brule, Pierre Radisson, and Louis Jolliet.

French Canadian Roots

Less likely is that you will find celebrities, people of common backgrounds who were famous in their time as poets, novelists, painters, architects, or scientists. Among the thousands of ancestors I have traced in my line I was only able to find a few – the designer of a cathedral, a great poet, and a man who was possibly the father of the 16th century soothsayer known as Nostradamus.

With certainty, I can tell you that some of your French-Canadian ancestors died of smallpox, and that they had children that died of this disease or other ailments. As I traced my family tree, I came upon one of my great, great… grandfathers who died of smallpox along with three of his children during the same epidemic.

As you push your ancestry into the 17th century, you will undoubtedly find that some of your ancestors were murdered… most often by the Iroquois (the indigenous arch-enemy of the early French Canadian settlers), some by the English (the other European power vying for control of the same part of North America), and some who perished at the hands of their own countryman.

The Ancestors You Don't Want to Know About

A few of your ancestors were unsavory characters. They were hung as murderers, or committed terrible crimes for which they were jailed or banished. Sometimes, you will wish you did not know about them.

Anja Osenberg

For me, there was Gillette Banne - my 10x great-grandmother, and also the first woman ever hung in what is now Canada. She poisoned her son-in-law and was executed in 1673.

Some of your fore-fathers and mothers may have participated in infamous court cases… like my 8th great-grandfather, Robert Paine. He was an Englishman, and the foreman of the jury that indicted those accused of witchcraft during the Salem witch trials in 1693.

I am related to Robert Paine through his grandson John, who was an English boy kidnapped as a child by the French during one of the many wars between the two colonial powers…who decided not to return to his old home after he was set free. (Note: for more on this aspect of colonial life, read the section later in the book called "Kidnapping in the Colonies")

Aside from the more colorful criminal trials that our ancestors were involved with, they also had civil disputes that went before the courts. The transcripts of these trials provide a glimpse into the daily life of how our relatives lived.

In fact, for most of our ancestors, it is only through their legal troubles that we have any details about their lives - aside from their birth, death, and land dealings - because court records of their brushes with the law were carefully preserved... whereas the deeds of your good ancestors went unrecorded, and thus we know very little about their daily lives.

"The unknown is always scary."

- Madeline Stuart

The New World

An Alien Place

It was like going to Mars. Except it wasn't a new planet your ancestors went to; it was a new and unexplored world here on Earth. And they were not just visiting; they were colonizing this alien place - settling permanently. But this other world was already inhabited, by people whom they mistakenly called "Indians", and some of those people did not like seeing the pasty white faces of your ancestors.

Some of these natives, like the Iroquois, were in league with the other European superpower trying to control this world… they were allied with the English who had deemed their part of the New

33

World "New England" just as most of your ancestors called theirs "New France".

The French Colonies in North America

The French colonies of North America

Though the number of colonists of English origin far outnumbered those of the French, the lands claimed by France encompassed not only Canada, but a vast part of what is now the United States as well. There were three major parts to France's dominion at the height of its colonization of North America: Acadia (now part of the Maritime Provinces of Canada and the state of Maine), New France (which at this time comprised the area from Quebec southward into Illinois), and Louisiana (the Mississippi valley if the United States). The latter was the biggest area by size, whereas New France was the biggest by population, and most of your ancestors will have hailed from there.

Since most of your French-Canadian ancestors will have lived their lives in New France, our discussion from this point on will focus on that area.

Populations overall, for all three territories, were small compared to those of the neighboring English. In 1666, during the first census ever taken in North America, the population of New France was just 3,215 people, and just 538 separate families. In keeping with our search for royal gateway ancestors, note that sixteen individuals were listed as "gentlemen of means", which I interpret as members of noble class.

Two-thirds of the people in France's colony were men, though the proportion of women was increasing through a program called "the King's Daughters."

"Arrival of the Brides" by Eleanor Fortescue-Brickdale

The "King's Daughters" were young women of good character who had fallen on hard times, usually due to the death of their father. Sometimes they were orphans. They came to the New World with a dowry provided by the king himself. Marriages took place soon after their arrival in New France, though they had a brief period where they could annul the arrangement and seek a new husband.

Despite the efforts to grow the population, by the mid-18th century New France still had only about 60,000 inhabitants, compared to two million in Britain's colonial dominion.

The British Colonies in North America

On April 10, 1606, King James I of England issued two charters, one each for the Virginia Company of London (often referred to as the London Company) and the Virginia Company of Plymouth, England (often referred to as the Plymouth Company). The London Company established the first successful British colony in Jamestown, Virginia in 1607. The Plymouth

Company did not fulfill its charter. (Note: do not confuse the Plymouth *Company* with the Plymouth *Colony*. They are two different things. I will discuss the colony shortly.)

Due to swampy conditions and widespread disease, someone died almost every day in the Jamestown colony. By September of 1607, more than 60 of the 104 colonists were dead. The settlers may well have died from drinking brackish creek water and from poor nutrition. One of the leaders of the colony was Captain James Smith who famously became friends with the native princess Pocahontas.

Depiction of Pocahontas saving John Smith of Jamestown

The Pilgrims

The English Pilgrims were members of the protestant Puritans, a Christian sect fleeing religious persecution in England who established Plymouth Colony in 1620, the first colony in the New England area and the second for the British in America (after Jamestown). The first of them came over on a ship called the Mayflower. Perhaps your genealogy can be traced to one of the 102 persons aboard this ship? We shall see.

Mayflower in Plymouth Harbor by William Halsall

A large influx of Puritans populated the region during the Puritan migration to New England (1620–1640), largely in the Boston and Salem area of what is now the state of Massachusetts.

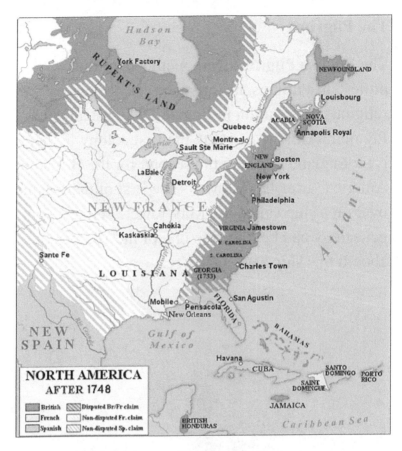

The British colonies and their neighbors in 1748

Other Neighboring Colonial Powers

Spain, the Netherlands and others all competed for control over the lands adjacent to those claimed by the British, but none competed more effectively and directly then the French, especially in terms of territorial dominion. That bitter rivalry culminated in a series of wars, including the French and Indian War which lasted from 1754 to 1763.

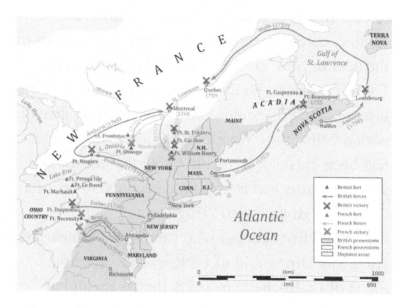

The 18th century "French and Indian War"

Why Did Our Ancestors Leave France?

There was a lot to survive in the New World if you made it there at all. A significant portion of the colonists died on the long voyage due to storms and disease. If you made it through that, there was a good chance that you would die from scurvy, from an assault by the Iroquois, small pox, or at the hands of the English.

French Canadian Roots

If you visit France today, a beautiful and peaceful land, you may ask "what motivated our ancestors to colonize such a hostile world?" Unlike the English colonies, religious freedom was not part of the deal in New France - you had to be Roman Catholic. After a hundred years of fighting between the Protestants and Catholics in France (a period called the "Wars of Religion"), the former had been crushed. It's quite likely that most of your ancestors had at one time been members of a Protestant group called "Huguenots", and descended from people who came from or near the Huguenot stronghold of La Rochelle. After the Siege of La Rochelle in 1628, they were all but destroyed, and those who survived were eventually compelled to become Catholic or die. Since you are here today, you are most likely descended from those who chose to live as Catholics – but remember that many of your kin were at one time protestant. If you are a devout Catholic today, as some of my relatives are, this is a bitter pill to swallow – yet it is the truth. The point here is that religious strife and constant war will have been fresh in the minds of those first pioneers who settled in the Americas.

16th century Calvinists burned for Protestant beliefs

To reiterate - the French port city of La Rochelle, and the outlying province of Aunis, will be the source of most of your ancestors. Aunis is in the ancient region known as Aquitaine which alternated between French and English ownership in the late middle ages (it was part of England's Angevin Empire until 1453). After the La Rochelle area, other regions in France that supplied many of your pioneer ancestors were Normandy, Perche, and Ile de France (i.e. the Paris area).

If you visit La Rochelle today, you may be surprised by how pretty the city and the countryside around it are. Aside from the constant warring and religious intolerance why would your ancestors leave this gorgeous place?

The harbor of La Rochelle, France

Some of your ancestors were probably thrill seekers and adventurers, but we have no direct evidence of this compelling people to leave for the New World. The more likely reasons for venturing to an alien world were the possibility of owning land and to a lesser extent the right to bear arms.

Historically land in Western Europe could only be owned by members of the noble class. Though some of your ancestors will have belonged to this class of people, it is more likely that most were commoners - peasants devoid of the right to own land.

Furthermore, the common people of France were not allowed to carry a pistol or a sword as this too was the exclusive right of the noble class. The right to bear arms was important at that time, as I personally discovered when I learned that one of my unarmed 17th century peasant ancestors died by the sword of a French nobleman.

In the New World it was possible for the lower social classes to own land and carry a sword – the latter necessitated by the constant threat of attack by the local Iroquois tribes.

It was for these reasons that your ancestor jumped on a boat, sailed for six weeks, and arrived in an untamed frontier place like Quebec City. If he or she was too poor to finance their own journey, they were indentured. An indentured servant is one step above being a slave. They had rights, but for a fixed period of time they had to serve their master, the person who financed their journey. After a number of years they were free to marry and establish a homestead - land of their own where they could build a house, keep livestock and farm. Once again, being armed was crucial, because they also had to defend their new land from the ever present risk of an Iroquois raid.

Kidnapping in the Colonies

Deerfield Raid – 112 English settlers taken to Montreal

Kidnapping was also a risk of life in the New World, with all of the parties involved (French, English, Iroquois, Huron) carrying each other's citizens off and ransoming them. Some of those kidnapped chose to stay with the kidnappers. A small number of your French Canadian ancestors will have English last names, or nick names (or even last names) such as "Langlois", French for the Englishman. They were most likely taken from New England as children, eventually freed, but chose to remain in New France where they ended up marrying into French Canadian families.

Life in New France

Life in 17th century New France was very different than it is today – aside from the perils I described earlier. For one thing, the families were huge. Not just because they were Catholic, but because the state had decreed it. As a father and mother you were fined if your daughter was 16, living with you, and - gasp - unmarried! A similar fine was levied if you had a son in a similar circumstance. Consequently people married young back then. It was not uncommon for a girl to be married at 13 or 14. Men would marry young too, but for them there was an expectation that they could support a family. Young couples in their early twenties had a large brood of kids already.

Disease was a constant companion. Small pox killed huge numbers of people. Sometimes it would claim multiple family members in a single season. Infant mortality kept parents in perpetual grief.

The End of New France

By 1759, France's time in the New World was coming to an end. On the Plains of Abraham, the principle city of Quebec was lost to the English and never retaken. The consequence of this loss was that it stemmed the tide of French colonists coming to the New World. The indirect consequence, and why it is relevant in the context of this book, is that any French Canadian ancestors that you have invariably had to have been in Canada by 1759, or in other words - you are assuredly descended from among the first European settlers of North America.

They Were Special

They did something special, these ancestors of yours. They traveled to a "Mars like" world, survived it, and thrived. They were the pioneers, and the fathers and mothers of Canada. It is for this reason that they are remembered, and it is for this reason that we - their descendants - can trace our family trees so well.

Furthermore, according to Discovery Magazine, the Roman Catholic Church in Quebec "has been a punctilious institution when it comes to preserving events under its purview such as baptisms and marriages. The genealogical archives are … robust" with "copious genealogical records."

Quebec's motto is "Je me souviens", which translates in English to "I remember"… and they mean it, literally.

Your ancestors struggled, toiled, and accomplished things that need to be remembered. They gave the world *you*. If you were here with me right now, I would raise a glass of wine high up into the air and propose a toast, "To our French-Canadian ancestors!"

"Give me six hours to chop down a tree and I will spend the first four sharpening the axe."

- Abraham Lincoln

On Your Mark, Get Set...

Now that you have some context – an understanding of why your ancestors left France, what they experienced, why we have such great records to work with, and what to expect as you explore, let's trace your family tree.

First, we will discuss the tools you will need; then, we will examine the resources available to help us; and finally, we will find out who your French Canadian ancestors were.

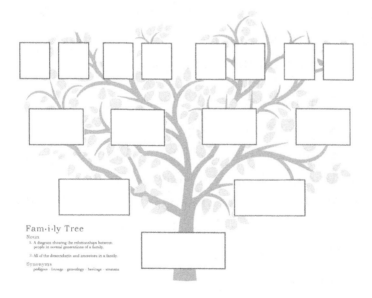

Fam·i·ly Tree

Noun

1. A diagram showing the relationships between people in several generations of a family.

2. All of the descendants and ancestors in a family.

Synonyms

pedigree · lineage · genealogy · heritage · stemma

Your Tool Kit

Before we begin, let's talk about the tools you should have to make your work easier.

First off, your computer will be your best friend in this quest. You will not only use the internet, but you will also need a database program to manage the vast numbers of ancestors that you will uncover.

Computer

First off, you need a computer. It will be your best friend in this quest. You will not only use the internet, but you will also need a genealogy program to manage the vast number of ancestors that you will uncover. Here are the minimum specifications for the machine you need:

- Pentium class PC or better.
- VGA or higher display.
- Windows 10 Pro or Home, Windows 8, Windows 7 (newer Macs must have Windows installed under Bootcamp, Parallel or Fusion . Linux machines will need a Windows emulator like VMWare or Sun's Virtual Box)

- A 32bit machine can suffice; however 64bit is an advantage because you will need as much processing power as you can get your hands on.
- A Hard Disk with at least 500 megabytes of available space.
- 8 GB of RAM minimum.
- A mouse.
- Plus, the computer must be capable of connecting to the internet.

When looking at the features of a computer to buy, choose processing capability over graphics, so go for "horsepower" - i.e. fast processors and lots of RAM. Graphics cards are not important, anything above VGA will suffice. The genealogy program that you will run is not graphically demanding, but it is a form of database software that will push your computer hard when you are processing thousands of records.

Some of you may want to start your record keeping using paper – that is how I started too. In an effort to stay organized as my family tree multiplied exponentially, I learned the age-old genealogical numbering technique of ahnentafel in an effort to keep things straight. Even with that method, it was hard to stay organized, simply because of the volume of information and the number of direct and indirect ancestors I came across in a short period of time. Eventually I decided to spend a modest amount of money on a genealogy database program, and my life became a lot easier.

It is probable that each of your French Canadian grandparents will yield between seven and twelve generations of direct ancestors stretching back into the seventeenth century. To determine how many ancestors you are going to end up with in your database let us do the math one more time, using ten generations:

Parents	2
Grandparents	4
Great Grand Parents	8
	16
	32
	64
	128
	256
	512
17 th Century	1024
Total Direct Ancestors	2046

Conservatively, you will end up with between 100 and 500 direct ancestors for every French Canadian grandparent you have. If any of the branches lead into a royal blood line, you may find your lineage stretching a full thirty generations, all the way back to Holy Roman Emperor Charlemagne – my 32nd Great Grandfather. This will add dozens, hundreds, and perhaps thousands more.

It is not surprising that I am a descendant of Charlemagne, and you most likely are too. The man left 18 children, some of whom became the heads of several European kingdoms, and they all had large families too. Plus, nobles were far more likely to survive pandemics like the black plague and small pox, unlike the common folk. As Adam Rutherford states in Popular Science magazine "if Charlemagne was alive in the ninth century, which we know he was, and he left descendants who are alive today, which we also know is true, then he is the ancestor of everyone of European descent... today." This assertion is also supported by math: if our number of direct ancestors doubles each generation, and Charlemagne was amongst our kin thirty generations ago, he was one of possibly a billion ancestors. There weren't even a billion people on Earth back then, but old Charlie can likely be found on many lines, as is the case in my own pedigree. (Royal families intermarried a lot, so marriages of their later descendants produced a bride and groom with the same great-grand parents. This is true, to a lesser degree, for the peasants as well)

Furthermore, Mr. Rutherford cites a mathematical calculation by Joseph Chang that estimates that everyone on Earth today is descended from one person who lived 3,600 years ago. In short, we are all cousins.

French Canadian Roots

In this book we will try to trace our ancestry as far back as possible - hopefully all the way to Charlemagne – and figure out who a few of our famous cousins are.

If you are serious about your search, and two or more of your grandparents are French Canadian, I urge you not to waste time with pen and paper – invest in a genealogy program. If you do not have two or more French Canadian grandparents, but you have grandparents who may be descended from the pioneers of the original thirteen English colonies, you will also want to invest in the proper software as well. The money you spend is well worth it.

Thus, for most of you, your tool kit will consist of the following:

- One computer
- Access to the internet.
- One software genealogy software program. I recommend a program called "Legacy Family Tree" produced by the Millennia Corporation.
- If you don't speak French, an online translation tool (like Google Translate).
- One first class plane ticket to France.
- Another first class plane ticket to Quebec.

If your partner wants to join you as you travel, get two plane tickets... though they are going to have to sit quietly while you analyze records in an archive for hours at a time... and they may have to fly economy because you only have enough money for one first class ticket, right?

The plane tickets are optional. The truth is that most of what can be found in the archives of France and Quebec is available on the internet, largely thanks to the efforts of the Church of Latter

Day Saints (LDS) who have gone to great lengths to scan, copy and safeguard genelogical records from all over the world. For example, I went to the archives in La Rochelle, France to find the marriage contract between my 10x great grandfather and his first wife. I found it, they were married back in 1644. To my dismay, I noticed that it had been stamped by the LDS as scanned into their records. All of their records are available online, so I knew that this part of the trip to these archives in France had been unnecessary. Had I througoughly searched the LDS's records I would have found it and saved myself a five thousand mile trip.

You may also find it easier to work with records on the internet than in an archive, simply because you can often copy and paste the records onto your computer, and paste the French text you find directly into a translation program such as Google Translate to get a quick English version of what you are reading. You can also use your computer to copy the photographs and scans that you find onto your own computer's hard drive. You cannot do this as easily with a paper document in an archive.

What is not optional is the genealogy program I mentioned. From this point on it is assumed that you have software that can handle the upload of genealogy files known as GEDCOMs (we will get to that later).

Resources

Now that you know what to put in your toolkit, let's examine the resources available to you. To do so, we will divide them between those that are online, and those that are not. Among the most important "offline" resources are your own relatives. They are the key to establishing the details of your grandparents and great-grandparents, for without them you may find it impossible to even get started, for such details often cannot be found "online". Visiting Genealogical libraries in person will also be a valuable "off the web" resource. Archives will be valuable both in person and on your computer.

Aside from harvesting knowledge from your relatives, libraries, and archives, most of your information will come from resources that can be found on the internet.

We will begin with the resources you are most likely to use first, so the starting point will probably be that one uncle or aunt who had an interest in your family's genealogy before you did. It is time to visit them.

"Talk to Aunt Marie"

Before you can use online research tools to push your pedigree back into the seventeenth century and beyond, you need to establish your more recent family tree. The only way you will be able to do this is by talking to living members of your family, in particular the eldest. Often there is an aunt or uncle that has taken on the role of family historian – so visit Uncle John or Aunt Marie.

After you visit the family historian, look towards your oldest living relatives. Are your grandparents still alive? If they are, engage with them to find out what they know about your family history. Do they have paper records and books they can share with you? Where were their parents and grandparents born? When, and what were their full names? Ask them to share their life stories, and those of their parents and grandparents, and then record it for posterity.

It is unlikely that you'll find your ancient ancestors online without knowing the specifics about the ones who weren't so ancient... and you will only learn this by talking to your eldest kin.

Talk to the elder members of your clan and find out what they know and what they have. Do they have a family history book? Do they have any birth, death, marriage or baptismal records? What do they remember about their grandparents? When talking to them bear in mind that you're in search of the where, when, and what of your ancestors…you want legal names (including middle), precise birth, death, and marriage dates, and the location of these events as well as that of where they resided. Carefully record this information even if it is only an allegation. Allegations are often true, though you should earmark these as such until they are proven.

Here is an example of an allegation: many years ago my aunt said we were related to mobster Al Capone's right hand man. In the course of my research, I investigated this notion and proved that we are not. In this case, the allegation was false.

Al Capone and his gang

Another assertion that proved to be false was that my maternal great grandmother was an orphan with unknown parents. This also proved to be false. However, sometimes these "leads" prove to be true, so they need to be investigated.

Once you have talked to the senior members of your extended family, gathered all of the family history books and paper records you can find, and you have a good idea of whom your great-grand parents were… it is time to record all of this information into the genealogy database program on your computer. After you have done this, we will go online and "turbo-charge" your search.

Download GEDCOM Files

Online resources are plentiful. However, the starting point is to scour the web for GEDCOM files for people of French Canadian descent. If you are not technically savvy, and the word "GEDCOM" sends shivers down your back, let me ease your mind… I will guide you, and make it as painless as possible.

First though, let's talk about why GEDCOM files are important, and why it is like attaching a rocket to your search.

Recall from the preface of this book that the main reason the librarian from the LDS Family History Library said we were lucky to have French Canadian ancestors is because our ethnic group has a well-documented and enviable family history. She was not exaggerating. Chances are that most of your family tree has already been researched by competent genealogists and that their work is available for you to piggy back on – complete with sources cited. Many have taken their research and made it available to share in a database file format that can be imported into most family tree programs. This file format is called "Genealogical Data Communication", known by the abbreviated term GEDCOM. It was developed by the LDS Church as a means to facilitate the exchange of genealogical data between different genealogy software.

Numerous GEDCOM files - containing the well documented pedigrees of French Canadians - are available on the web. Sometimes you will have to ask the owner of the data for permission to download it, sometimes it will be free and accessible. All you have to do is gather the appropriate ones, and arrange the information in your own database.

But is it accurate information?

Let me tell you this: genealogists are a fastidious sort, hell-bent on accuracy, especially those who choose to share their work using GEDCOM files... so rest assured that their records are almost always accurate. Though you will occasionally find errors, they are far and few between. You must, however, stay vigilant and examine the work you are thinking of importing critically before deciding to incorporate it into your database. Even after you have done the import, you must stay vigilant to keep your work error free.

The bigger challenge is that everyone's family tree is different, so you will have to grab many files to assemble your own. This will require that you "scrub" your database to prevent duplicates after every GEDCOM download. Once again, I will show you the process later in the book.

What is the payback for learning how to use GEDCOM file formats? In a single hour, after finding a file containing seven generations in a branch of your family tree, you could end up with 250 well documented and well sourced direct ancestors added to your pedigree. In addition, you may find hundreds of indirect ancestors – the brothers and sisters of your forefathers and mothers. These indirect relationships are the key to establishing who your famous cousins are. Are you related to Queen Elizabeth II, Angelina Jolie, or Justin Bieber? Probably… and the indirect relationships that get imported in GEDCOM files are the key to finding out.

Queen Elizabeth II

In summary, GEDCOM files allow you to get a running start by downloading the work of other genealogists. In order to get this running start you must purchase a software package that is capable of loading them. A leader in this area is Legacy Family Tree by Millennia Corporation. You can purchase their product online and download the program. From that point you can trace your French Canadian ancestors, find pedigrees that have a GEDCOMs available, and download parts of your pedigree to fill out your tree.

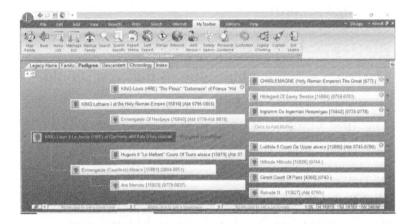

Pedigree view in Legacy Family Tree

Legacy software can be purchased on the web at:

legacyfamilytree.com/downloadlegacy.asp

You can download a free version to begin with, but you'll soon find that the reasonable cost of the deluxe version makes it a good value proposition.

The combination of GEDCOMS and Legacy software will quickly yield a large portion of your French Canadian Family tree – on the order of 80%. The other 20% will be much harder, and take up far more time than you spent assembling parts of your trees by loading files from made available by other genealogists. This will be the part where you go where few other genealogists have gone before, digging into actual birth, death and marriage records.

PRDH Database

There are a few leading sources that you should check out when you have a gap in your family tree. The first place to start at is the University of Montreal. They run a project known as "The Research Program in Historical Demography", also known by the acronym "PRDH". It requires a subscription fee, but it is reasonable and a great value for your buck Access it at:

genealogie.umontreal.ca/en/home

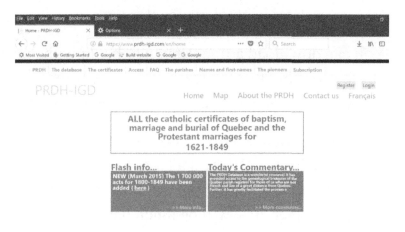

PRDH Home Screen

Thankfully for us Anglophones, the site has an English portal. You can switch to that version once you enter the site for the first time. The screen print displayed above is after you have switched the language to English. After selecting your preferred language, you must register.

As mentioned earlier, the PRDH is a subscription based service, and unique in that regard in that you do not purchase an amount of time that you can use the site, but rather an amount of "hits". The site explains that a " 'hit' is used every time a record certificate, an individual file, a family file or a couple file is viewed. The original search that leads to the result list is free." You buy blocks of hits, as per the following price list effective summer 2018:

Number of hits	Cost before taxes	Cost per hit
150	24.15$	16¢
500	43.95$	9¢
1000	71.45$	7¢
2500	140.75$	5.5¢
5000	208.95$	4¢
10000	347.55$	3.5¢

Prices are in Canadian dollars ($CAD)
Quebec residents: + GST + QST
Canada residents outside of Quebec: + GST + PST
Residents from outside Canada: No taxes

The bottom line is that a subscription to the PRDH is a good value proposition – you may go years before exhausting your "hit" supply. I bought a thousand hits in 2013, and have only used up two-thirds… five years later.

Here is PRDH's own description of the certificates contained in on their site –

> "The PRDH data base includes some 2 400 000 certificates of various types, dated from 1621 to 1849. The vast majority correspond to the systematic extracting of information from records of baptisms, marriages, and burials that came to us from the parishes, missions, and Catholic institutions in Quebec that kept registers before 1850. Are also part of the data the 26 000 Protestant marriages recorded before 1850. The certificates were read and transcribed onto magnetic media according to a standard format that reproduces the essential information contained in the documents: type, place of registration, and date of the record; family names, first names, and characteristics of the people cited as the subject of the act, as their parents or as spouses. The documents for the period

1621–1765 include all of the individuals cited, thus including witnesses; beyond, they are generally not included, because it appeared preferable to favor the number of certificates."

In the PRDH, you will find almost every legal and church document concerning your ancestors prior to the 19th century. This provides you a snapshot of your ancestor's whereabouts, family, and legal dealings (including land transactions). They also maintain a list of "pioneers" that can be useful to determine who of a line was the first to arrive in what was then known as the colony of New France.

Once you subscribe, you can search for information regarding your ancestors by following the menu path <Access < Member Access

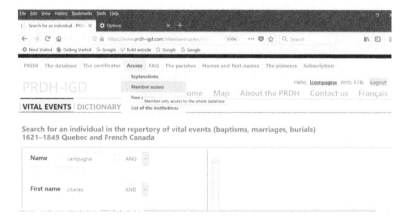

In the example below I have entered the information for "Charles Campagna", the first of my line born in the New World.

Pressing on the search button yields 66 records, including Charles' baptism in 1668.

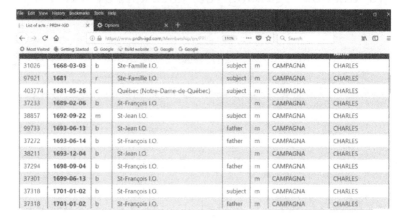

B = baptism, m = marriage, r = census, c = confirmation

The second record is from the 1681 census. It records that Charles is a 14 year old boy living with his parents. Note the discrepancy in the spelling of the last name. As you do your research, keep in mind that surnames can have many variations. In my case the potential spellings are Compagna, Campagna, Campagnard, and Campagnat. The alternate spellings may be the result of illiteracy, since many of our ancestors could not read or write. However, another culprit maybe language itself, since for many of our "French" ancestors their first language may have been something like Occitan or a dialect like Saintongeais. It is possible that French was a second language for some of the first of your line to immigrate to the New World, thus contributing to the differences that you may see in the spellings of last names.

Census

#97921

Ste-Famille I.O.

Vers 1681

Rank	Name	Age	M.S.	Pr.	Sex
01	**MATHIAS CAMPAGNARD** Occupation : HABITANT Residence : STE-FAMILLE I.O.	050	m	p	m
02	**SUZANNE ROBINEAU** Residence : STE-FAMILLE I.O.	047	m	p	f
03	**CHARLES CAMPAGNARD** SON OF 01 Residence : STE-FAMILLE I.O.	014	c	p	m

In summary, if you find yourself with a gap in your French Canadian family tree, I strongly suggest that the first place to try and remedy this problem is the PRDH.

The second place is the Ancestry.com web site.

Ancestry.com Website

For a fee, Ancestry.com allows users to access the extensive collection maintained by the Church of Latter Day Saints. They have gone to great lengths to scan and preserve genealogical records not only in Canada, the United States, and France… but all over the world. If you have a gap in your family tree, and it could not be filled in by using PRDH, you may find what you are looking for on this site. Ancestry is particularly useful if some of your ancestors are not French Canadian. On this site you are likely to uncover scans of birth certificates, marriage certificates, and baptismal records from all over the world. You can then download them, and flesh out your family tree. However, in general this will only work for ancestors who have been deceased for at least thirty years or so. It has a very robust search engine. The initial search screen is shown below.

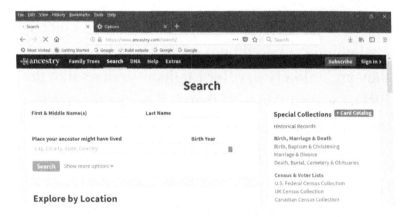

The types of records you can find on Ancestry include immigration, census, voter lists, grave location, records of birth, marriage, and death, some travel information (border crossings for example), Military, as well as public member trees.

Departmental Archives of France

When you reach the first person in a line to have immigrated to the Americas, you will need to continue your search in France. This is particularly true if the subject made that initial journey sometime after the French lost the colony of New France in 1759. In such cases, most of your online research may take place in a department's archives in France. Fortunately for you, this will not be the case for most of your ancestors, because the vast majority arrived in the New World prior the 1759.

Research using departmental archives in France is challenging if you do not speak French because they are unlikely to offer English versions like the PRDH website does. If that describes you, use a translation program to assist you (refer to the section concerning translation programs).

If you are researching ancestors who immigrated to North America prior to 1759, the majority of your kin will have originated in the Charente Maritime Department in France. There are other regions that also provided large numbers migrants to the New World (Normandy for example), but none more so than Charente Maritime, which incorporates the city of La Rochelle, the port city from which most of your ancestors would have departed Europe from.

In my case, three out of four of my grandparents are from pioneer families - those Europeans that first settled the Saint Lawrence River region of North America – while one of my grandfathers is from a family that came to the Americas in 1905. Coincidentally, even this recent immigrant came from the Charente Maritime Department, just like most of my ancestors who made that same journey by sea several centuries before him.

Later in the book, I will demonstrate the use of the "Archives en ligne", i.e. the online archives of the Charente Maritime Department.

Before I do, be forewarned that the progress in these on-line French archives will be slow compared to what it is when working with the records for those old French Canadian pioneer families, because everything you do will be primary research. Generally, you will be doing research that few others have ever attempted.

The first step after you determine the region of France that you believe your ancestor came from is to locate the web page for their archives. In my case, I searched "Charente Maritime archives en ligne". The website address is:

https://archives.charente-maritime.fr/

At this point, we will digress to a discussion of the use of translations programs to aid our research. Later in the book, I will demonstrate a search.

Translation Programs

Though the PRDH online database and Ancestry.com website are available in English, many of the documents you encounter will be in French – for example the scans of original baptismal, burial, and marriage records. In addition, you may find yourself having to use a French only website such as that of an archive in France. If you are not fluent in French, use an online translation tool to help you understand what you are looking at. Below is a link to Google Translate:

https://translate.google.com/

One function that is particularly useful with Google Translate is its ability to translate entire web pages into English. In order to do that, simply type in the full website address including the http part, and then click on the link it provides in the

English panel on the right side. The original French language page of the archives is shown below:

Original Website in French

The website after using Google Translate now shows in English:

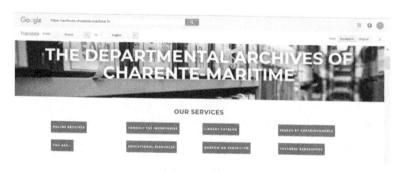

Website after Translation into English

The Quebec Royal Descends website

You will use the "Quebec and Acadian Royal Descends" page from a website called "Genealogy of the French in North America" (GFNA) to help you identify the ancestors in your line who were, or may have been, members of the French nobility. A royal connection is the key to pushing your genealogy back into the middle ages.

The GFNA website address is:

http://www.francogene.com/gfna/gfna/998/qrd30.htm

 Genealogy of the French in North America

Genealogy of the French in North America

Quebec and Acadian Royal Descends (QRD30)- Main references

This table is a list of immigrants having a king among their ancestors. The list is mostly about immigrants coming from France and who spent at least one winter in North America, or that settled (during at least one year) in a former French colony of the North American continent. This list is not limited to the province of Quebec but to the diocese of Quebec as defined in the 1750s (i.e. Acadia and Louisiana are included). Also, if a royal immigrant came with siblings or children, they are also included.

Valid lines with or witout descendants in North America (proven or likely correct until proven wrong)

Background colors mean:

• Green: I have descendants after 1899 in my database or I know descendants or I know that descendants exist
• Blue: otherwise
• White: main reference about that immigrant

Notes: links are to family sheets. To find the king, you have to travel from one family to another by moving the mouse over the parents or parents-in-law. The number of additional generations will be shown.

GFNA Royal Descends Homepage

Though this database is comprehensive, it is possible for you to have a noble ancestor who is not listed, particularly in the case of one who did not immigrate into Canada.

Google Books

Google provides a great service in its ongoing effort to scan rare books and make them available online. Among the volumes that are now available online are old genealogical works of tremendous importance. You can find books concerning both French Canadian and French genealogy that can help you piece together your family tree.

These invaluable books are particularly helpful if you have a line of nobility in your tree, because there are many ancient books concerning the pedigree and heraldry of the French aristocracy. In my opinion, the most helpful of these is "Dictionnaire de La Noblesse", which is a multi-volume work by Francois De La Chenaye-Desbois published in 1786. Google has the collection available online and available to download in PDF format.

DICTIONNAIRE

D E

LA NOBLESSE,

CONTENANT les Généalogies, l'Hiftoire & la Chronologie des Familles Nobles de France, l'explication de leurs Armes, & l'état des grandes Terres du Royaume aujourd'hui poffédées à titre de Prihcipautés, Duchés, Marquifats, Comtés, Vicomtés, Baronnies, &c. par création, héritages, alliances, donations, fubftitutions, mutations, achats ou autrement.

On a joint à ce Dictionnaire le Tableau Généalogique, Hiftorique, des Maifons Souveraines de l'Europe, & une Notice des Familles étrangeres, les plus anciennes, les plus nobles,& les plus illuftres.

françois Alexandre Aubert

Par M? *DE LA CHENAYE - DESBOIS.*

SECONDE ÉDITION.

TOME X.

A PARIS,

Chez ANTOINE BOUDET, Libraire-Imprimeur du Roi, rue faint Jacques.

M. DCC. LXXV.

AVEC APPROBATION, ET PRIVILEGE DU ROI.

The Dictionnaire de La Noblesse - 1786

Archives and Genealogical Libraries

Only rarely will you have to go in person to an archive to uncover the branches of your family tree because the records of most large archives are online. However, occasionally it will be required because there are small archives throughout

Quebec and France that are not on the web, for which a trip in person is worthwhile.

As mentioned earlier, the majority of your ancestors will have come from the La Rochelle area, which is now in the Charente Maritime Department of France. The documents contained in their archives can be searched at:

http://www.archinoe.net/v2/ad17/registre.html

Even when an archive has its records online, it can still be worthwhile to visit them just to look through their book collections. Often they will have volumes and volumes of genealogical dictionaries that list out family trees for many generations. They also have books that add historical context to your search.

Due to their extensive book collection, I also recommend a visit to the Family History Library in Salt Lake City at least once in your life, preferably after you have fleshed out most of you family tree to the 17th century... because knowing the details of your pedigree will make the trip more meaningful and allow you to make maximum usage of their books.

"I am from there. I am from here.

I am not there and I am not here.

I have two names, which meet and part,

and I have two languages.

I forget which of them I dream in."

— Mahmoud Darwish

Discover Your Pedigree

The Steps

Now that you have a good idea of the resources that are available to you both online and offline, we will go through an example step-by-step. The steps are:

1. Establish your great-grandparents by talking to your kin.
2. Use GEDCOM files found on the web to accelerate the process of building your tree.
3. Look for royal gateway ancestors to push your line into the middle ages.
4. Fix those broken branches.
5. Start over at Step 2.

In the first step we will determine whom all of your great grandparents were - their full names, where they were born, married and died, and on what dates. We will then record all of this information in our genealogy program.

In the second step, we will use GEDCOM's from the web to piggyback off the work of other genealogists to accelerate the process.

In the third step, we will look for ancestors who were part of the "ancient regime", i.e. the old noble class of France.

In the fourth and final step, we will fill in the missing pieces by using the PRDH database, Ancestry.com, and one of the online departmental archives in France.

Now, let's walk through the steps in a make-believe case study.

An Imaginary Example

Now, imagine...

The Rumor

You have heard a rumor from a relative that you are a remote cousin of Canadian Prime Minister Justin Trudeau. This stimulates your interest in learning about your family tree. Is it true or not? Aside from Justin, do you have any other notable ancestors? Then you start to think about these mysterious ancestors of yours. Who were they? Where did they come from? Where did they live? What did they do for a living? How long have your "people" been in North America? Why the heck did they leave Europe in the first place?

23rd Prime Minister of Canada – Justin Trudeau

Step One – Your Great Grandparents

You have already purchased a suitable computer, bought the Legacy Family Tree database program (or one of their competitors), done the tutorial, and your work space is connected to the internet… and now you are looking for advice on how to uncover these mysterious ancestors of yours. The first thing you need to do is determine who your great grandparents were. You will not be able to do this online; you will have to talk to your relatives to figure this out. So you talk to an Aunt who shares what will soon become your obsession. She has a book that shows that one of your great grandparents was named Jean Charles Emile Trudeau.

He was born way back in 1874. He represents 1/8th of your total pedigree, because you have seven other great grand-grandparents. You are going to have to repeat the process that follows for the other seven, but for now - and for the purposes of this book - you will trace the lineage of Jean Charles only. As you discover information you will diligently record it, along with the source.

Step Two – GEDCOM Files

Though it may seem daunting, the value of learning to use GEDCOM files makes it very worthwhile to learn – even for the technically challenged. Be patient, and understand what the payback is – hundreds of well researched direct and indirect ancestors in short amount of time.

Thus, the second step to perform, after you have established ancestors into the nineteenth century (i.e. your great-grandparents), is to look online for a pedigree that has a downloadable GEDCOM. There are many websites available that allow you to download these types of files, including Ancestry.com (you'll need permission from the owner), Rootsweb (being revamped at the time of writing), and others. Just search the internet and you will find sources.

Assuming that you followed my earlier advice, you bought a genealogy database program that will serve as your repository for the information you gather from these GEDCOM files as well as your own personal research.

Assuming you have located a good genealogy database on the internet that has at least some GEDCOM's available: in the surname field you enter your imaginary ancestors last name "Trudeau", and in the Given name simply "Jean".

Going back to our example the result of an online query for "Jean Trudeau" is daunting – with many records representing an assortment of individuals from four different centuries and several countries. You will need to be more specific. All you know about Jean's wife, your grandmother, is that her name was Grace. You cross reference your search with this name and far fewer results are shown. Furthermore, the birth date for both records says "After 1874", and you happen to know that your great grandfather was born in 1876. Eureka! You have found your line of descent.

Do any of the records you found on the web have a GEDCOM available? Some records have it available, and most do not. In this case, you are in

luck, because a mouse click on each record shows
that some do. Which one should you choose? You
click on "Download GEDCOM" on each page.
One reveals that the number of generations
available to download is ten, while the other is six.
You may be tempted to immediately download the
larger file, but before you do, examine the quality
of each tree by looking at a sample of individuals
in each. Which has better sourcing? Which has
more extensive information, and which has more
direct ancestors shown? You pick the second
record for a number of reasons: you can download
ten generations, the number of ancestors shown
exceeds that of the first even in the first six
generations shown, and it goes further back (see
figure below).

I am sitting right next to you and I point out that the decision is not mutually exclusive. You can download both, but you have to be careful because doing so could lead to a large number of duplicate records requiring a lot of clean up. I suggest that you proceed with the download of the second record, after which we'll discuss what we should do with the other record. You are a little nervous, but you click on "Download GEDCOM".

"Don't worry" I tell you. "You can't break anything." *At this point,* I think to myself.

You accept all of the default settings and click "Download." A few seconds later, the information now resides on your hard drive.

Next, I tell you to open your genealogy program (as mentioned previously, all of our examples assume that you invested in Legacy Family Tree).

In a previous step, you entered yourself, your parents, your siblings, grandparents, and your great grandparents. Aside from this, the database is empty.

With my guidance, you open the data you just downloaded using the following menu path:

File<Import<GEDCOM

Then you proceed with the import. A panel opens up stating that 328 individuals from 200 families are included. Accepting all of the defaults you click on "Start the import." A message tells you that you've been successful, and asks if you want to merge duplicates now. The answer is no, because aside from the family members you entered the database was empty. After you import the other GEDCOM, you will have to merge the duplicates it finds.

After the import is complete, I look over and say to you, "Congratulations! You just established the identity of over two hundred direct ancestors. Furthermore, you've pushed your family tree into the 17th century... and you may have a few lines that we can push even further into the past with...look at how this branch leads to a lady named Anne Convent – born 1601, died in 1675." (Refer to Figure 5).

"The Arrival of the French Girls at Quebec, 1667", by
Charles William Jefferys

Later in the book, I'll tell you why people like
Anne Convent are so important.

After studying your results in your genealogy
program, I suggest that you return to the web and
look at the first record of the two (the one that we
decided was inferior).

"Compare it to what you downloaded," I urge. The
comparison yields one unique branch. "Check the
quality."

You do, and find that it looks reasonable and is
well sourced.

"Click on the top node of the unique branch and download that GEDCOM."

Following the directions, you repeat the earlier process. This time, however, you click on the duplicate checking functionality immediately following the import into your genealogy program. A few duplicates are found, and you follow the instructions of the software and merge them. Thirty more direct ancestors are added to your database, along with their siblings, vital statistics, a few stories about them, and the sources of the information – it took about twenty minutes.

The beauty of having French Canadian ancestors is that their lines are usually well known all the way back into the early seventeenth century; the people involved are well documented; plus, well-researched GEDCOM files abound.

After this initial success, I instruct you to return to the original record on the web so that I can show you something I noticed earlier. "Look at the children of Jean and Grace."

Three are listed: Suzette, Jean Charles, and Joseph Philippe - who had the nick name… "Pierre!" we both say in unison.

"Pierre Trudeau?" you reply incredulously, "Thee Pierre?"

15th Prime Minister of Canada – Pierre Trudeau

"Yes," I nod - the iconic, flamboyant, and tough 15th Prime Minister of Canada... and the father of the current leader of Canada, Justin Trudeau.

Your head snaps back as if someone just shoved your forehead.

Step Three – Look for the King and Queen

Using your genealogy program, it takes you about twenty minutes to link your great-grandparent with the last name Trudeau (i.e. Jean Charles) to Joseph Philippe.

Assuming you are using the Legacy Family Tree program - In the pedigree view… right click on Add<Parents<Link to Existing Parents and search for Jean and Grace. When you find them, click on Select.

Voila! Your family tree now contains over 230 direct ancestors along this branch alone, because you just attached this line to your own.

"Go back to that second record," I say.

You click on it, and expand the tree view. "Scroll down to the bottom." (See figure 5). I point to a record for Anne Convent/Couvent. "Do you have her in your database?"

You downloaded ten generations, and having been born in 1601 she's in danger of having been missed. However, in this case you have had some luck, because she was the tenth and final generation imported... so she's in your records. If she was not, you would have to do another download to include her.

"Go back to the web and click on her name," I say.

After you do so, Anne Convent's details emerge. She was born in D'Estrees, France in 1601 and died in Quebec City on Christmas Day, 1675. You also notice the lengthy list of source citations, the first being Tanguay Volume 1.

"Looks legit" you comment as you continue reading. I agree with you – Cyprien Tanguay was a respected authority on French Canadian genealogy back in the nineteenth century.

Then you notice the second citation.

"... research by Roland-Yves Gagne and Laurent Kokanosky have linked Anne Couvent (spelled on many sites Convent) back to Robert, comte d'Artois, son of King Louis VIII"

CHARLES 1ᵉʳ DUC DE VENDÔME 1515

A Depiction of King Louis VIII

"Seriously, King Louis VIII?" you remark.

"Yes. Anne Convent is well known in French Canadian genealogy circles" I reply. "She's what is called a 'royal gateway' ancestor. From her, you can push your genealogy back into the middle ages. She was a direct descendent of Charlemagne."

"Who?" your mouth is slight agape.

"Charlemagne. He was a king who lived in the eighth or ninth century… actually, he was the Holy Roman Emperor. He's considered the ancestor of every European royal family today. Some say he was the greatest king who ever lived. You've never heard of him?"

"Of course I've heard of him, I was just testing you," you tease.

This demonstrates step three - look for members of French nobility because they are gateways into the distant past, long before your ancestors arrived in the New World. Aside from Anne Convent some of the names to watch out for are: the Leneuf brothers, Hellene De Belleau, and Catherine De Baillon.

A good source of royal gateway people is the GFNA - Quebec Royal Descends website. It can be found here –

Francogene.com/gfna/gfna/998/qrd30.htm

They have an extensive list of French Canadian royal gateway ancestors along with a critical opinion as to their validity.

For now, though, the important thing is to add Anne Convent's tree to your burgeoning one. Remember that you were only able to download ten generations, and she was the tenth. As we are still looking at the web record I instruct you to click on Anne's Pedigree view. The screen explodes. Another ten generations of your direct ancestors pops up, going back to the fourteenth century.

"Download the GEDCOM," I urge excitedly, "if this pedigree is complete, you're going to have to grab these ten generations, as well as the next ten, and the next ten after that. You may have thirty generations by the time you're done, and hundreds more direct ancestors. By the end of today, your database will have thousands in your pedigree, and you'll know some of your ancestors going all the way back to the ninth century!"

After you download the GEDCOM, add it to your growing database, and run the duplicate checking program, I tell you to return to the online pedigree for Anne Convent.

"Click on that person... Jean VI de Ghistelles," I request, pointing to an individual who died sometime after 1414. You do so, and his pedigree explodes before us.

Then I tell you to click on Henry I, Margrave of Nordgau, who died in 1017. Once again, an extensive family tree branch is exposed, this one showing the icon himself... Charlemagne.

"See that guy?" I ask pointing to Charlemagne's grandfather Charles Martel.

You nod, "Yeah?"

"Because of him, you're a Christian instead of Muslim." As you turn your head to look at me, I notice a wrinkle appear on your forehead and your eyes narrow. "... At the Battle of Tours, he destroyed the Islamic invasion which until that point looked like it was unstoppable. The Muslims had cavalry, and the French did not, they were all on foot. The strategy that Charles Martel used was so effective that it is still studied in military school today. 'The Hammer' was his nickname."

Charles "The Hammer" Martel – Battle of Tours (Charles
de Steuben's "Bataille de Poitiers en octobre")

You notice that Charles Martel was born in 688.
"How far back can we go? Can we get back to the
time of Christ?"

"Sort of. Along this line we can get a few more
generations beyond Charles Martel, all the way to
his great grandparents - Pepin and his wife Saint
Itta, but this is about as far back as we can reliably
go. You're talking about a concept called 'descent
from antiquity'... the idea that we can trace our
ancestry back into ancient times, like to the
Romans. Saint Itta is likely a direct descendent of
some Roman senators going all the way back to
the 4th century AD, but it can't be proven.
But…there is another possible line for Europeans
that goes through one of the crusader knights, a

guy named Balian. There's a movie about how he defended Jerusalem with like a dozen knights, it's called 'Kingdom of Heaven'. The descent into ancient times is actually through his wife, who has an ancestry that goes back to before Christ, but it is not proven either. It is an intriguing thought, because most of her pedigree looks pretty solid."

"Crusaders? Knights?"

"Yes, you'll probably have a few in your family tree. It's time for me to go home though. Can you download these GEDCOM files on your own?"

You answer in the affirmative, so I leave you with your homework. "Tomorrow we'll discuss how to fix 'broken branches' in your tree. Good night."

Step Four – Fixing Broken Branches

The next morning, I return. You have dark circles under your eyes – a true sign that obsession is setting in. "Were you up late last night?"

"Yeah. I was just reading about some of these people in my family tree."

"Interesting, eh?"

"Yes. It was still daylight when I started. When I looked up it was night," you say with a chuckle that turns into a yawn.

"I've been there." I try not to yawn in sympathy, "Now, let's have a look at what your family tree looks like now."

French Canadian Roots

You open your family tree program, and as we study your pedigree together I point to the end of one of the branches in your tree, "Do you see how this line ends at this lady?" I have to stop myself from tapping the screen. I hate it when people tap on my computer screen. "We need to work on that."

"Okay," you reply, "What do we do?"

"There are a couple of things we can do. We could travel to Montreal to look for her, but that isn't necessary at this point."

"Especially given that she's dead," you remark dryly.

I look at you with a smile and shake my head, "We can find her records online. We don't need to fly to Montreal. There's an easier way, and if that doesn't work there is another way that's a wee bit harder."

"What's the easy way?"

"Since she lived in the 1700's we can find her on the PRDH."

"What's the PRDH?"

"The PRDH is the website of a genealogy project conducted by the University of Montreal. They maintain this online database that is well researched and super reliable. However, unlike the website you previously used, you have to pay for this service. Luckily, you're a billionaire, right?"

We both look at the stack of bills next to your computer. "… don't worry. It won't cost much."

As I grab coffee from your kitchen, you enter your credit card information to subscribe to the PRDH service.

Returning, I set two steaming mugs down on the desk.

"Now what?" you say.

With my left hand I make a go forward motion "See if you can find her."

You locate the lady who is a dead end in your family tree... and her parents are shown. "Enter the information into your program."

After you do so, and establish the proper links, I encourage you do be a good genealogist, "Don't forget to cite your sources."

As you type a note into the record you created for her stating that you found this information in the PRDH you remark, "Why do I need to cite my sources?" It seems like a waste of time to you. "I'm doing this just for fun."

"One day, you may look back at this record and question its accuracy… because maybe some other source that's less reliable than the PRDH will say something else. This note will give you confidence in your records. Plus, one day you may download it to the web as a GEDCOM so that you can help other genealogists, and they'll take comfort knowing that this information came from a reputable source."

"Fine," You're tired from your late night and lack of sleep. This feels a little too much like work, but you enter the information anyway. "Now what?"

"Eventually you'll return to the web to see if there's a GEDCOM for these pair you just found - this lady's parents… but for now let's look at another broken link." The next one you look at is your great-great-great grandmother Marie Catherine Longtin. She died in 1778. In vain, you try the PRDH website.

"Nothing. I guess that's it." I can see that you are ready to slam the screen of your laptop shut. Your eyelids look heavy.

"You're going to give up just like that?"

"What else can I do?" I can see that you are thinking about a nap.

"Ancestry.com"

"But if these guys don't have it, why would Ancestry?"

"Trust me, try their website." You type in the website address, and it asks for some of that unlimited money supply you have. A six month

115

subscription costs on the order of a hundred bucks, depending on the options you choose. After entering your credit card information, I urge you to enter her name, plus that of her husband (your great grandfather) in the query tool for Marriage Records. You enter an approximate year for the marriage that is likely +/- within ten years. You get a direct hit, and within moments you are looking at a scan of their old marriage document, dated February 17, 1749 (see below).

You ignore the surname discrepancy – by now you understand and accept that spelling variations abound in the world of genealogy. Expanding the view of the attached document you notice that not only did the bride and groom sign, but it also bears the signatures of their parents. The quality of the scan is excellent, as is the penmanship of all the signatories. From this document you can clearly tell who Marie Catherine Longtin's parents were - These were your great, great, great … grandparents. As you look at their signatures your mouth is once again slightly ajar. It is a special moment when you see the handwriting of your ancestor who signed a document hundreds of years ago. You update your database.

As I leave your house, you are searching the web for GEDCOM files for the two new sets of great-grandparent's you uncovered today. You barely notice me leave.

Meanwhile... Back in the Old Country

A week later, and I'm over at your place again. You have made great strides in your project – your documented pedigree now consists of several thousand direct ancestors. But you are wearing a frown on your face as you talk about your current status.

"I'm stuck in this one area," you say as you roll back your office chair and plunk yourself in front of your desktop computer. You navigate through your genealogy software to a fellow named Paul

Chalifour. Paul was born in 1612 in La Rochelle, France; probably a survivor of the infamous siege that killed the majority of the population of that city in 1628. He is your eight great-grand father through his son Paul Jr.

You point to the screen, to where his wife should be. "Isn't that strange? I can't find any mention of this wife anywhere. The GEDCOM files I downloaded don't contain her. Ancestry and PRDH say nothing. What can I do?"

I put my hands on my hips, and look out the window. My eyes are looking at nothing, when I notice a hawk up in the sky surveying the landscape below. That is when an idea pops into my head. "Primary research," I say turning back to meet your expectant gaze.

"Okayyyy," you reply. "What does that mean?"

"Much of what you've done so far has been gathering and assembling the pedigrees of your French Canadian ancestors whose genealogy has been well researched. You haven't had to do very much in the way of *primary* research... the type of work you do when you have to look at old records in an archive. In our case, you don't have to go in person, because the place that holds La Rochelle's old records - Charente Maritime Department Archives in France - is online. Let's try to find a record of his marriage in their archive. If we can find it, his spouse will be shown."

I direct you to their website, https://archives.charente-maritime.fr/

Earlier, in the Translation Programs section of this book, we translated this page into English. To actually work with it, we will do so in the original French version because it functions better as you drill into it. You keep another browser open with the translated version of the webpage so that you can toggle between it and the original.

"Click on 'LES ARCHIVES EN LIGNE'," I instruct (see the picture above). After you do so I say, "Good, now click on 'Etat Civil'." (see picture below)

119

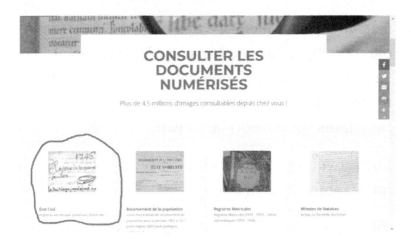

"What does 'etat civil' mean?" you ask.

"Etat civil translates to 'civil status'. It is a repository of vital information such as births, deaths, and marriages."

After you select Etat Civil, the following screen pops up on your computer.

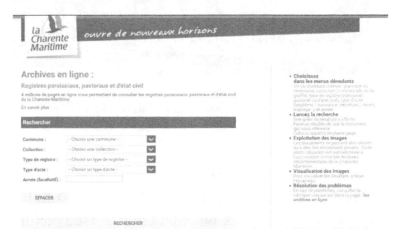

In this example, Paul Chalifour is from La Rochelle, so enter that in the Commune field. In France, Communes are like the townships and municipalities in North America. In the Collection field, "Greffe" translates to "Registry", while "Communale" refers to the records of the Communes. You may also see other possible choices such as hospitaliere, which means hospital records.

If the record you were searching for was after the French revolution of 1789, you would search for "Etat Civil" in the "Type de Registre" box (i.e. type of register). However, if the record you seek likely pre-dates the revolution as is the case with Paul marriage, pick "Paroissial", which means "parish". These are the records administered by the Roman Catholic Church who carried out this function before the government of France became more secular. Enter the suspected marriage year, and leave all other fields blank as shown below.

At the bottom of your screen, "Effacer" literally means "Wipe off". Use Effacer to clear the selections, and "Recercher" to research the database.

Below is what the screen appears like after filling it out with information that I believe will lead us to the marriage record we seek:

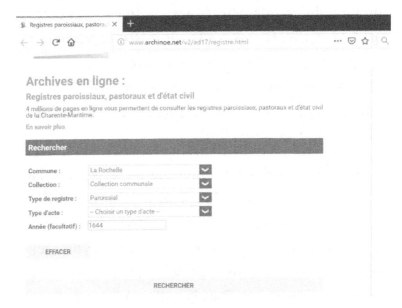

Clicking on Rechercher yields a lengthy list of document links, as shown below:

G G 183	La Rochelle	Collection communale	Paroissial	Sépultures	Pas de table	Paroisse Saint-Barthélémy	1630 - 1650
G G 182	La Rochelle	Collection communale	Paroissial	Baptêmes	Pas de table	Paroisse Saint-Barthélémy	1630 - 1655
G G 182	La Rochelle	Collection communale	Paroissial	Mariages	Pas de table	Registre relié à l'envers - Paroisse Sal...	1630 - 1655
Non coté	La Rochelle	Collection communale	Paroissial	Tables décennales	Table chronologique	Paroisse Saint-Barthélémy	1630 - 1669
Non coté	La Rochelle	Collection communale	Paroissial	Tables décennales	Table chronologique	Paroisse Saint-Barthélémy	1630 - 1669
Non coté	La Rochelle	Collection communale	Paroissial	Tables décennales	Table chronologique	Paroisse Saint-Barthélémy	1630 - 1792
G G 352	La Rochelle	Collection communale	Paroissial	Baptêmes	Pas de table	Paroisse Saint-Jean-du-Pérot La paroisse	1632 - 1654
G G 352	La Rochelle	Collection communale	Paroissial	Mariages	Pas de table	Paroisse Saint-Jean-du-Pérot	1632 - 1655
G G 377	La Rochelle	Collection communale	Paroissial	Sépultures	Pas de table	Église Sainte-Marguerite	1605 - 1665
G G 376	La Rochelle	Collection communale	Paroissial	Mariages	Pas de table	Église Sainte-Marguerite	1636 - 1664

There are three that contain marriage records. Each will have to be checked.

My friend offers up this additional piece of information, "According to my info, Paul Chalifour was from a part of La Rochelle called Perigny."

I study the list again. Unfortunately, "Perigny" is not found, so we have nothing to narrow our search down. "You're going to have to go through all three of the marriage links to try and find out who his wife was."

You groan, and at this, I decide it's time to leave you and your computer alone for an hour and go for a walk.

*****

I come back an hour later, and enter through the unlocked front door to find you still at your computer. The smile on your face tells me that you must have had some success. "Let me see his marriage record."

You hand me a document that you just printed.

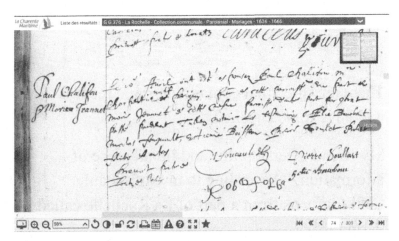

"You did it! You found their marriage, and his wife… Marie Jeannet. Well done. He was a charpentier… a carpenter. What is the name of the register you found it in?"

You point to your computer screen where I see the cover of the register.

"Oh my goodness," I exclaim.

"What?"

"The La chapelle Sainte-Marguerite… the church they were married in. It is still standing! I went to a mass there a few years ago… if you go to La Rochelle, you can stand in the exact same spot your ancestor was married in 350 years ago!"

La Chapelle Sainte-Marguerite, La Rochelle, France

"Now then, wasn't that easy?" I jibe.

"Um... no, it was kind of hard," you pause in reflection, "but when I finally found the record, it was pretty awesome." You manage a smile that I return.

Step Five – Start Over

Genealogy never ends. When you get to this point, return to Step Two and start over. Try to find more GEDCOM files to improve your family tree. By doing this you will end up with information regarding many of the siblings of your ancestors. This will allow you to more easily determine your relationship to famous people (see the section called "Discover Your Cousins"). You will also get additional details about your ancestors by harnessing the efforts of other genealogists through the GEDCOM files they share.

From Step Two, you will continue on to through the other steps, ever improving your family tree.

What Should You Expect?

If you have French Canadian ancestors, the method in the preceding example will have several results.

First, with enough diligence, you will discover *every* French Canadian ancestor born after the year 1600. This assumes that all of the branches in your family tree lead to individuals who were already in the New World at the time of the 1666 Census of New France - 3,215 Europeans, in 538 families were counted in North America's first ever census, and invariably… almost all French Canadians can traces their lines to this relatively small group.

The above is true if none of your lines has orphans, indigenous people, or "late comers" to New France. Recall that France's dominion over this part of the world was over by the 1759. In that year, the French lost Canada when it lost the Battle of the Plains of Abraham to the English. Thus, 1759 is effectively the last year that your French Canadian ancestors could have immigrated to the New World from the old. Consistently, though, you will find that your pioneer forefathers and foremothers arrived in the seventeenth century.

The second result you can expect, especially if all four of your grandparents were French Canadian, is that some of your lines lead to "royal gateway" people such as Anne Convent. From noble ancestors such as Anne, you'll be able to push your family tree all the way back to Charlemagne in the eighth century.

Another result you can expect is that you will uncover several thousand of direct ancestors. There will be so many that their management requires that you have a proper database system such as Legacy Family Tree. The majority of these records will have been found with relative ease, thus the decision to invest in proper software at an early stage is prudent.

Descent from Antiquity

The Charlemagne Connection

Pushing one's roots back to ancient times is considered the "holy grail" of genealogy. By ancient times we mean prior to the Middle Ages, which began after the fall of the Roman Empire in the late 5th century. Such a pedigree is referred to as a "descent from antiquity", or DFA for short. Unfortunately no verifiable DFA - one that has been accepted by scholars - has ever been produced. Many claims have been made going back almost to the dawn of the medieval period when royal families fabricated their ancient lineages, but none have ever been proven with contemporary corroboration at each generation.

That being said, there are many proposed roots and some may one day be proven. If you are of European descent as I am, the route will likely go through the iconic Holy Roman Emperor Charles the Great, also known as Charlemagne, who was born in approximately the year 742 somewhere in Belgium or Germany (historians are not exactly sure of the location).

If you are European you are most likely a descendent of Charlemagne. As I mentioned earlier in this book, it is not far fetched to assume that most Europeans are descended from him. He was prolific, having left 18 children, and many of them became the heads of several European kingdoms. Couple this with the increased ability of royal families to survive the black plague and small pox as compared to the serfs, and it becomes more likely to be descended from him than a commoner.

Earlier I cited Adam Rutherford who stated in Popular Science magazine "if Charlemagne was alive in the ninth century, which we know he was, and he left descendants who are alive today, which we also know is true, then he is the ancestor of everyone of European descent... today."

If you can find royal gateway ancestors in your family tree, it is most likely that "Chuck" can be found along many lines, as is the case in my own genealogy. Multiple branches leading to Charlemagne occur because the royal families of Europe intermarried a lot, so once you tap into a royal ancestor you will see the great man along many lines.

However, Charlemagne is not the furthest that Europeans can travel back along their family trees. As I mentioned earlier, his grandfather Charles Martel was illustrious in his own right, having single handedly preserved Christianity in Western Europe by turning back a hitherto unstoppable Islamic invasion in the year 732 at the Battle of Tours.

However, we can push our European pedigrees back even further than Charles "the Hammer" Martel, for he himself was the well documented son of Pepin II of Herstal and his second wife Alpaida, who was in turn the son of Ansegisil and Saint Begga (a lady who became a nun after the death of her husband and the birth of several children). The parents of Begga were Pepin of Landen and Saint Itta of Metz, a lady who was born sometime around the year 592. To this point, the genealogy is accepted by scholars with documentation and contemporary sources to support it. Unfortunately no parentage can be proven for either Pepin or Itta.

This means that for most Europeans, *Saint Itta of Metz and her husband Pepin are the furthest back that we can reliably push our ancestry.*

Any attempt to go further back then Itta and Pepin is speculation, because no proof exists at this time.

Saint Itta (592 to 652 AD)

However, it is likely that Itta is the daughter of Arnoald, the Bishop of Metz, though no direct record of this relationship has ever been found. Assuming that Arnoald was her father, this is *a*

132

gateway point into a descent from antiquity - in this case a link to ancestors who lived in the ancient Roman Empire - because Arnoald was the progeny of Roman senators and politicians.

Arnoald of Metz was the son of a Gallo-Roman senator named Ansbertus, who in turn may be the great grandson of Tonantius Ferreolus who lived from about 390 to 475. Tonantius was the Roman praetorian prefect of Gaul. His father was Ferreolus, Tribune of Gaul, and a Roman Senator, who in turn was the grandson (via his mother) of the 4th century Roman politician and administrator Flavius Afranius Syagrius. Flavius became Praefectus Urbi of Rome in the year 381 and a Consul in 382.

If this is correct, this Citizen of ancient Rome known as Flavius was my 45th Great Grandfather. If you are European, *he may be yours too.*

This is my unproven, though probable, case for a descent from antiquity through Charlemagne.

Significance

What this means to readers of European descent is that if you can find a legitimate royal gateway ancestor in your tree and tap into one of the old noble families of Europe, you can prove your lineage all the way to Charlemagne. Once you are in his line it traces to his grandfather Charles Martel, whose line can be traced all the way to his great grandparents Itta and Pepin, who lived in the early 7th century. From there you have a shaky ancestral line going all the way back to senators of the late ancient empire of Rome.

Returning to our example, you will find that Anne Convent is a direct descendant of Charlemagne along many lines (Ermentrude of Auxerre for one), and therefore a descendant of Saint Itta and Pepin of Landen… and maybe even a descendant of some Roman people.

Middle Eastern

There is an alternative argument for a descent from antiquity that goes through the Middle East. If it proves correct, it goes several hundred years further into the past then the line that goes through Charlemagne.

Balian II of Ibelin was a crusader knight who lived in the 12th century. If you have European blood you may find him in your family tree. If you find a royal gateway ancestor with ancient roots, you will find him in your tree, for he is the ancestor of the Kings of Cyprus, England, France, Scotland, and Germany.

If you are a movie buff, Balian is the subject of a 2005 movie called "Kingdom of Heaven" featuring Orlando Bloom in the lead role. It tells the true story of Balian's epic defense of Jerusalem during a siege by a 20,000 man Islamic army. With only 14 knights at his disposal, Balian was able to push the battle to a draw.

Balian is not the source of this descent from antiquity; it is through his wife that he marries while in service to the King of Jerusalem. Her name was Maria Comnena. She was the daughter of John Doukas Komnenos, a senior member of the Byzantine Royal Family, and Maria Taronitissa, a descendant of the ancient Armenian kings.

Through the ancient Armenian royal family we link to what is known as the Bagratid line.

Working from the earliest ancestor in this family tree, the route starts with the Parthian King Arsaces I, the first of the Arsacid dynasty. He ruled from 247 BC to 217 BC. One of his descendants, king Tiridates III of Armenia, who reigned early in the 4th century, is known to have been an ancestor of Nerses the Great. The latter's son Sahak I was the father-in-law of Hamazasp I, an Armenian ruler from the Mamikonian dynasty. Then the line can be traced, though not with certainty, to a much later Mamikonian, Samuel II of Armenia, whose son-in-law was Smbat VIII Bagratuni, Constable of Armenia and forefather of all the living Bagratids. The advantage of this route is that its crucial links (from Arsacids to Gregorids, from Gregorids to Mamikonids, and from Mamikonids to Bagratids) may be corroborated by near-contemporary sources, dating to within a century after the key marriages took place.

My published family tree shows that I am the 68th great-grandson of Arsaces. In other words if this highly speculative pedigree is correct, he is my direct ancestor from 70 odd generations ago. However, the key point in this DFA (like all others) is that it cannot be completely corroborated. It is possible and interesting, but far from proven. That being said there is an interesting person that emerges from this line that takes the speculative aspect from interesting to fun.

An assertion has been made that the Armenian Royal family married into that of the descendants of the great Zenobia.

Queen Zenobia's Last Look upon Palmyra by G. Schmalz

Zenobia was the Queen of Palmyra who lived in the 3rd century AD.

Zenobia was a striking woman. In the Roman publication "Augustan History" written by an unknown author in the 4th century AD she is described:

> "Her face was dark and of a swarthy hue, her eyes were black and powerful beyond the usual wont, her spirit divinely great, and her beauty incredible. So white were her teeth that many thought that she had pearls in place of teeth."

Zenobia wasn't just a pretty face; she was smart, bold and brave. Among her accomplishments was leading the army of Palmyra in a victorious invasion of Egypt in 270 AD. She supported her claim to the land by claiming that she was a direct descendant of one of that land's most famous women.

In the *Augustan History*, Zenobia is said to have been a descendant of Cleopatra and claimed descent from the Ptolemies.

What does this mean for you? It means that if you can find a royal gateway ancestor from an old European family and establish a connection to the famous crusader night Balian II, you will have established a connection to the Armenian royal family. Once you have established that connection, you have tapped into the tenuous claim that they intermarried with the family of the great Queen Zenobia. You then become part of Zenobia's own claim to be a direct descendant of Cleopatra.

The Meeting of Antony and Cleopatra by L. Alma-Tadema

Not only will you have Cleopatra in your family tree, but you will have tenuously pushed your family tree to a man who lived 23 centuries ago – Arsaces.

Other European DFAs

Many other DFAs have been put forth, including one that goes through the Portuguese (also via the Armenian royal family), another through Attila the Hun (by connecting him to Charlemagne), and still another through the Welsh Kings (known only from an inscription on a Welsh pillar that connects this royal family to a descendant of a Roman Emperor).

The Muslim Connection

Descendants of the prophet Muhammad (who was born in the late sixth century) are plentiful, and because of the tax and social benefits accorded them, many claims are false. One such claim was made by my 11th century Iberian ancestor Zaida of Seville. She was unique in that she was a refugee Muslim princess who was first a mistress and then later possibly the wife of the Christian King Alfonso VI of Castile.

Before her association with King Alfonso, Zaida is said by Iberian Muslim sources to have been the daughter-in-law of Al Mutamid, the Muslim King of Seville, wife of his son Abu al Fatah al Ma'mun, ruler of the Taifa of Córdoba, (d. 1091 AD).

141

Zaida was one of those who claimed descent from the prophet Muhammad, who lived from 570 to 632 AD.

"A Moorish Maid", by John Lavery

I am not alone in my descent from the Moorish princess Zaida, as demonstrated in this article published on October 10th, 1986 from United Press

International titled *Moslem's in Buckingham Palace*:

> "Mixed in with Queen Elizabeth's blue blood is the blood of the Moslem prophet Mohammed, according to Burke's Peerage, the genealogical guide to royalty. The relation came out when Harold B. Brooks-Baker, publishing director of Burke's, wrote Prime Minister Margaret Thatcher to ask for better security for the royal family. 'The royal family's direct descent from the prophet Mohammed cannot be relied upon to protect the royal family forever from Moslem terrorists,' he said. Probably realizing the connection would be a surprise to many, he added, 'It is little known by the British people that the blood of Mohammed flows in the veins of the queen. However, all Moslem religious leaders are proud of this fact.'

As mentioned, social privileges and immunities accorded to descendants of Muhammad have led to a vast quantity of false declarations of their lineages. Similar to other parts of the world, claiming noble ancestry helped reinforce a ruler. In the Ottoman Empire, tax breaks for "the People of the House" encouraged many people to buy certificates of descent or forge genealogies; an Ottoman bureaucrat estimated that there were 300,000 impostors; in 18th-century Anatolia, nearly all upper-class urban people claimed descent from Muhammad. The number of people claiming such ancestry—which exempted them from taxes became so great that tax collection was very difficult. The Hashemite kings of Jordan the Alaouite kings of Morocco, and the Aga Khans, all claim descent from Muhammad or his close relatives.

Like all of the other DFAs mentioned, Zaida's lineage to the prophet cannot be proven.

"No matter where we come from, there is one language we can all speak and understand from birth, the language of the heart, love."

— Imania Margria, Secrets of My Heart

Discover Your Cousins

Now that you have uncovered your entire French Canadian family tree, you can go one step further. Aside from Trudeau, who are your cousins? Some people find this more fun than finding out who your ancestors were. Finding out that the movie star Angelina Jolie is your fifth cousin, or that pop star Justin Bieber is your seventh cousin twice removed can be great entertainment. If you can prove that your distant cousin is Queen Elizabeth, perhaps you will be invited to dine at Buckingham Palace?

Step One - Finding Subjects

You probably know some of your first cousins. You may even know a few second cousins. But amongst your more distant cousins… are there any celebrities? Are there any famous political figures? How about sports hall of famers? Are there any infamous relatives that are best left uncovered? Sometimes the ancestors who were best forgotten become those we want to remember. Were there any pirates, any slaves or slave holders, or any murderers?

If you know that someone famous has at least some French Canadian ancestry, there is strong likelihood that you are related to them if you go far enough back in time. People that have such ancestors include:

- Hillary Clinton, former U.S. Presidential candidate,
- Camilla Parker Bowles, the Duchess of Cornwall and Wife of Prince Charles
- Madonna, pop star
- Celine Dion, French Canadian songstress
- Mario Lemieux, NHL Hall of Famer and owner of the Pittsburgh Penguins.
- Brett Favre, NFL Hall of Fame quarterback

Hall of Fame NFL quarterback Brett Favre

All of the celebrities mentioned above may be related to you. If all four of your grandparents are French Canadian, it is almost assured that they are.

Though she does not have French Canadian ancestry, Queen Elizabeth II of the United Kingdom does have French ancestors. If you can take your pedigree back far enough you may find a link between the two of you.

Step Two – Find Their Grandparents

The process for establishing a direct connection between you and a celebrity is similar to that which you followed when you established our own ancestry. Once you have a target, you have to establish that person's pedigree. Their parents can usually be found on their Wikipedia article. Occasionally even their grandparents are listed. You'll have to be creative on the internet to push their lineage into the nineteenth century. If you're lucky, the targets family tree will be listed on the web. One place to check is the website "Famous Kin". It can be found at:

https://famouskin.com/

Step Three – Find GEDCOM Files

Once you've pushed the target's pedigree into the nineteenth century, follow the same steps that you used to establish your own ancestry. Be sure to load the GEDCOM files you discover along the way into your database. Also, be wary of duplicate records as you may have many. Run the duplicate checking program of your software after every load.

Step Four

After you've discovered the celebrity's lineage, found GEDCOM files, downloaded them into your database, and removed duplicate records… you are ready for the final step - establishing your relationship with the celebrity target.

To do this use the relationship checking function of your genealogy software. In Legacy Family Tree, the relationship calculator can be found in the menu under <Tools <Relationship

Expected Results

If your hunch turns out to be correct, you will be able to establish a connection between you and the target celebrity. Typically, amongst people with French Canadian ancestry, they will be somewhere between eighth and tenth cousins of yours. Occasionally, it will be even closer. For example, Angelina Jolie is my sixth cousin, because we are both direct descendants of the same great-great grandfather who died in 1838.

If you count Queen Elizabeth II as a cousin, it is likely a far more remote relationship that dates back into France before the colonization of Canada - in my case Liz (as I like to call her) is a 14th cousin. She's almost beyond "distant".

A Word on Relations that are "Removed"

There is often confusion as to what "removed" means when it comes to your relatives. As it says in the glossary, it refers to a relationship separated by a particular number of steps of descent, i.e. by generation. Here is an example:

My mother has a much older sister. As a result of the age gap between them, my Mom has a niece by this sister who is the same age as her. We shall call her "Bethany". Because of Bethany's age, she seems more like an aunt to me, but she's not. Despite the fact that she is so much older than me, she and I are the same generation relative to our grandparents. She is my first cousin. Age wise Bethany is my mother's peer, but she is the daughter of my mom's sister; they are one generation removed from one another. Bethany is the same generation as me, but from an age perspective she is *not* my peer.

Bethany has a daughter named Roxanne who is exactly my age. Roxanne seems like my first cousin, but in fact it is her mother (Bethany) who is my first cousin. She is one generation further removed from my grandfather – her great-grandfather. *Relationships are measured against those who are of the same generation,* so her mother (Bethany) is my first cousin. Some might think this makes Roxanne my second cousin, but as you will see shortly, she is not. Roxanne is my first cousin once *removed.*

To show why I am not Roxanne's second cousin, one only needs to look at someone who *is* – my son. My grandfather is the great grandfather to both Roxanne and my son. *They are of the same generation.* My son's second cousin (Roxanne) is my first cousin once removed.

Here is a graphic that might help clarify:

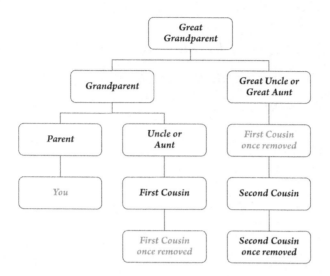

Example of "removed" in family relationships

"England and France were rivals, not only on the continent, but in the West Indies, in India, and in Europe."

- Albert Bushnell Hart

English Roots

Since the French colonies in the New World existed side-by-side with those of the English, and because the histories of both countries have been intertwined ever since William the Conqueror of Normandy took over England in 1066, you may find points of intersection in your family tree that mean that some of your ancestors were English.

There are several scenarios that explain your English ancestors.

Kidnapped!

At various times in the history of colonial North America, the English and French used kidnapping as a tactic during their many wars with each other. They would kidnap, and then ransom each other's citizens. (Refer to the section in this book called "The New World").

Both sides did it. They raided each other's settlements and carried off some of the inhabitants.

The relevance to us as genealogists is that some of the kidnapped English colonists chose not to return to their native land after they were set free by the French, and they ended up marrying into French Canadian families and becoming our ancestors.

An example of this occurred as a result of the 1704 raid during Queen Anne's War when French and Native forces attacked the English frontier settlement at Deerfield, Massachusetts taking 112 settlers captive to Montreal. Some died along the way and sixty were later redeemed (ransomed by family and community). In this period, the English and their native allies were involved in similar raids against villages in New France where they were doing their own abducting, ransoming… and killing. Some of the events were particularly brutal, such as the Lachine Massacre of 1689, which may have resulted in the loss of life for as many as two-thirds of the town's French inhabitants.

Some of the English captives remained in New France by choice for the rest of their lives. This is particularly true of many of the younger captives, who were adopted into French Canadian society. 36 Deerfield captives, mostly children and teenagers at the time of the raid, remained permanently. Those who stayed were not compelled by force, but rather by newly formed religious ties and family bonds. Captive experience was largely dictated by gender as well as age. Young women most easily and readily assimilated into French Canadian society. Nine girls remained as opposed to only five boys. These choices reflect the larger frontier pattern of incorporation of young women into Canadian society. These young women remained, not because of compulsion, or a fascination with outdoor adventure, or the allure of life in a foreign society, but because they transitioned into established lives in new communities and formed bonds of family, religion, and language. More than half of young female captives who remained settled in Montreal where "the lives of these former Deerfield residents differed very little in their broad outlines from their former neighbors." Whether in New France or in Deerfield, these women generally were part of frontier agricultural communities where they tended to marry in their teens or early twenties and have six or seven children.

If you find an ancestor who started life off in the English colonies, you'll have a pedigree that may lead to some interesting characters from early American history. In my case, it led to Robert Payne, my 8x great grandfather…and also the foreman of the grand jury that led to witchcraft indictments in Salem, Massachusetts in 1693. In my great grandfather's defense, the only evidence of his participation was that he returned findings of "Ignoramus", a legal word meaning uninformed. It is written on a bill by a grand jury, when they find that there is not sufficient evidence to authorize their finding it a true bill. Sometimes, instead of using this word, the grand jury endorses "Not found" on the bill.

The Salem Witch Trials

The Norman Conquest of England

The earliest point at which your family tree will intersect with those of the English only applies if you find royal gateway ancestors. A small percentage of your 17th century kin will fit into this category.

The intersection of French genealogy with that of the English results from William the Conqueror's conquest of England in 1066.

William was a Franco-Norman who was also the Duke of Normandy on France's Northwest coast. The result of his victory in the Battle of Hastings was several hundred years of Norman rule over England, creating a situation where the official language of the royal court of England was in fact French. Even after the Norman influence over England ended (after several centuries), the English royal family continued to marry with those of the French nobility.

The result is that your pedigree - if you've been able to find "royal gateway" ancestors among the French Canadian pioneers (e.g. Anne Convent and the Leneuf family) - will intersect with the English during the late middle ages. Undoubtedly you'll count the prodigious King Edward the First of England, a man of French descent with numerous offspring, as your ancestor. He is portrayed below left as the villain in the movie Braveheart.

Amongst the Norman elite of England was Richard the Lionhearted, as well as several generations of Anglo-Norman monarchs. You'll also find the tyrant King John, who was forced to sign the Magna Carta in 1215.

The Angevin Empire

The marriage of the English / Norman King Henry II to Eleanor, the Duchess of Aquitaine, led to what became known as the Angevin Empire…with its centerpiece Eleanor's inheritance of the entire land of Aquitaine, in what is now a big chunk of southwest France.

Eleanor, Duchess of Aquitaine

As mentioned earlier in the book, the La Rochelle area of France is the source of most of your French Canadian ancestors – and it was located in Aquitaine. From Eleanor's time until 1453, the area belonged to England. Add to that the fact that Normandy was itself a major source of our French Canadian ancestors. Thus, if you find any royal gateway ancestors you will often find many English in their family trees from the high to late middle ages (i.e. from 1066 until about the year 1500).

There is also another interesting byproduct of extending your family tree to the Norman/French rulers of England. Using your genealogical software you can establish your precise relationship to Queen Elizabeth, Prince William, Princess Diana, and the rest of the present monarchy of the United Kingdom. However, do not expect to be invited to the next coronation as you are likely on the order of a 14th or 15th cousin.

The British royal family

"Never forget the three powerful resources you always have available to you: love, prayer, and forgiveness."

- H. Jackson Brown, Jr.

American Huguenots

If you are American, you probably know the story of Paul Revere and his famous ride, right? Well, just in case you don't (or you are Canadian), here is what happened:

The midnight sky was pitch black on April 18th, 1775 as Paul Revere rode his horse through the New England countryside warning the American Patriots that the "British are coming". His journey became legendary and is commemorated in the Henry Wadsworth Longfellow poem "Paul Revere's Ride".

Paul Revere's Fateful Ride

If you are lucky enough to find Paul in your family tree you might be surprised to find out that his father Apollos had emigrated from France to the colonies. Apollos was one of the thousands of Huguenots who came to the New World.

"Emigration of the Huguenots" by Jan Neuhuys

As mentioned earlier in this book, the Huguenots were a Protestant denomination that is virtually extinct due to persecution. Unlike their counterparts who migrated to New France, the American Huguenots were not required to Abjure and become Catholic. Thus, there has never been a Huguenot presence in Canada, though a small number of the group survived in the United States.

In my work building French Canadian family trees, I have only rarely come across a situation where someone from a Catholic French Canadian family intermarried with a French Huguenot family from the British colonies. Just keep in mind that while most French pioneer families came through New France, a few (like Paul Revere, the son of a Huguenot) came through on the British side without ever having live in French controlled North America. One of their communities in New York state is named New Rochelle, after the place in France where many of your ancestors originated – La Rochelle.

Additional Resources

Aside from what I have mentioned in this book there are plenty of other resources that are worthwhile. The Family History Library in downtown Salt Lake City is fantastic. Like most of the archives I've come across their records have been digitalized and are available on the internet. The real value is in their huge library. It is several floors, although the French Canadian book section is relatively small compared to other sections. The staff is extremely helpful if you need assistance in your search.

An additional website is also worth mentioning. It is called "Jamie Allen's Family Tree & Ancient Genealogical Allegations." Assuming you find a "royal gateway" ancestor in your tree (if all four of your grandparents are French Canadian it is almost assured), Jamie's portal will both entertain and may even assist you. Very few of the pioneers of New France are on the site, but when you have a "gateway" ancestor this site can help you navigate the royal world before 1500. You can compare your tree to Jamie's for accuracy and to help when you have hit a road block. Be cautioned that this website is not error free, but in most respects it is reasonable. You can find it at Fabpedigree.com.

"We are all migrants through time."

— Mohsin Hamid, Exit West

A Note on French Canadian Ancestry versus European

Three quarters of my ancestry is "old" French Canadian, descended from those first European settlers in Canada…the ones who arrived prior to the Battle of the Plains of Abraham in 1759. The other quarter emigrated from France to Canada in 1905. After great success tracing my Canadian ancestors, I thought that the French side would be a treasure trove for a genealogist. I was wrong.

Our descent from people who have done great things is remembered, whereas it tends to be forgotten without memorable people in one's line. The French Canadians descended from illustrious pioneers, the brave men and women who colonized a world that was as alien to them as Mars is to us.

"Radisson arrives at an Indian Camp, 1660"

On the other hand, my more recent French ancestors were grape farmers who had no pioneers or celebrities in their family tree.

Furthermore, Europe has repeatedly been decimated by war resulting in the destruction of invaluable genealogical records, whereas Canada never suffered this fate. For example, before retreating from the French city of Caen at the end of World War II, the Nazis burnt the archives to the ground. It contained 14,000 books relating to the ancestry of Caen's inhabitants.

What I discovered, the hard way, is that it is often impossible to trace the lineage of ancestors from Europe more than a few hundred years. At the very least, it is much more difficult than it is when compared to the ease with which you will trace the lineage of the French-Canadians who descended from those original pioneer families that settled the New World.

"Genes are like the story, and DNA is the language that the story is written in."

-   Sam Kean

DNA Testing

The Decision to Get an Ancestry DNA Test

You have probably seen the advertisements on television.

"Discover your family tree. Do you want to know who you are? Well, just send us a saliva sample and we will tell you everything you want to know."

I had done some research that suggested these tests are accurate in determining if you have some native blood, if you have Europeans, Africans or Asian in your family tree, or if some of your ancestors were Jewish. However, according to what I had read, the ability of these tests to differentiate between ethnic Caucasian groups (e.g. whether you were Slovenian, Norwegian, French, or Italian) is questionable.

For the purposes of writing this book, I decided to try one of the testing services. Since my main motivation is genealogy, I decided to use Ancestry.com's service known as AncestryDNA.

I bought a kit, spit into a small vial, and sent it through the mail to a facility in Ireland.

Initial Results

About a month later I received the results. This is what they looked like:

Ethnicity Estimate	Updates ❶ ⌃
Ireland/Scotland/Wales	31% >
Europe South	22% >
Scandinavia	19% >
Iberian Peninsula	17% >
Great Britain	6% >

The results did not look right at all. From my genealogical research I knew that my ethnicity was about as French as one could possibly be, yet that ethnicity wasn't mentioned at all. So, I tried to rationalize these numbers.

I knew that the majority of my ancestors came from the La Rochelle, France area, so I researched the ethnic make-up of that area. It turns out that the indigenous tribes of that area at the time of its initial occupation by the Roman Empire two millennia ago were Celtic. Since the Irish, Welsh and Scots are considered the "modern" Celt regions, I concluded that the highest ethnicity estimate was in essence "Celtic", not Irish / Scottish / Welsh.

The remainder of the numbers did not surprise me. Most of my ancestors were from Southwest France, near the Spanish border, so Europe South and Iberian make sense. The second leading source of my ancestors was the Normandy area of France, a region that had been colonized by the Vikings. The word Normandy itself is derived from the word "Northman".

One thing I found odd about the results is that French ethnicity was not mentioned at all. *Curious.*

"Migrations" was something that the test did get right; it detected that I was descended from the French settlers of the Saint Lawrence River area of North America – in other words, the people who populated the colony of New France in the 17th century.

Ethnicity Estimate

Updates ⓘ ︿

Migrations

◉ **Saint Lawrence River French Settlers**   ›
From your regions: Great Britain; Ireland/Scotl...

◉ Beauce, Québec, French Settlers

As shown above, these French settlers are still connected to the regions of Great Britain, Ireland and Scotland.

The results of the test were what I expected. It confirmed that I am white, but not much more than that.

However, these were preliminary results that raised more questions than they answered. I did not realize that more refined results were on their way. Take note of the "Updates" button in the upper right hand area of the picture above. The science behind DNA testing for genealogical purposes is really more of an art, and as time goes on the people behind it are improving. Consequently you should check for updates to your DNA profile often, because it may change.

Updated Results

A few months later I logged back into Ancestry's DNA portal and was notified that my results had been updated. It now looked completely different…and very accurate; it confirmed what I knew all along from my genealogical research – I am almost completely French. Ancestry DNA assessed the figure at 92% (the range was between 88 and 100%).

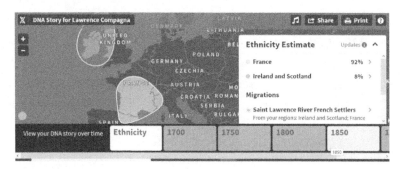

Ethnicity Estimate   Updates ⓘ ∧

⬤ **France**   **92%** ›

⬤ **Ireland and Scotland**   **8%** ›

The 8% Irish and Scottish is somewhat of a mystery, but as I had already determined, the original inhabitants of the area of France that my people came from were Celtic, so that might

179

explain it. The other explanation was that one of my French lines was not so French after all. I welcomed this anomaly, as it would cause me to reexamine my pedigree to ensure its accuracy.

The Migration area of the results didn't change, though it now included the word "France", though it was listed second to Ireland and Scotland.

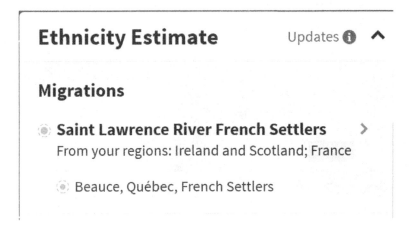

Relatives

Another byproduct of getting the test done is that I received messages from people who were related. One was a third cousin; another was a sixth cousin.

In the DNA Matches area of the AncestryDNA, I was surprised to see a list of over 1,000 people that were my first, second, third, or fourth cousins. My Aunt and first cousin headed up the list. I even recognized the names of some of the second cousins; I had met one of them. I didn't know any of the third or fourth cousins, though a few of the last names were those of the people I was familiar with in my family tree.

After the update, the Ancestry DNA test was accurate. Its ability to determine my relation to people like my aunt and cousins was impressive.

One thing that AncestryDNA did not show was my relation to people who are famous, infamous or notable. That would be interesting.

"Wherever you go, go with all your heart."

\- Confucius

Take a Trip

Travel for Context

You do not have to leave the comfort of your own home to do the bulk of your genealogical work, because most of your primary research can be done using the internet. Most of the records you are looking for have been scanned and are available online.

As I mentioned earlier in this book, I once went to the Charente Maritime Archives in La Rochelle France, excited about the discoveries I was about to make there. I did find a record of my ancestor's wedding in 1631, but at the same time I noticed that it had stamped as scanned and preserved in the digital archives of the Church of Latter Day Saints (LDS). Since Ancestry.com contains LDS records in their website, I suspected that it had not been necessary to travel all the way to France to just to see this. Later, at the hotel I was staying at, I got on my computer and confirmed what I suspected – this ancient marriage record I was so excited to find in a French archive was available online. Every record I found there was in fact available on the web. From this perspective, this trip seemed like a waste of time.

But it wasn't.

The true value in going to France, as well as to Quebec, is that you learn the historical context for those dry records that you're compiling. For example, before I went to France I did not realize the extent to which my ancestors were Huguenots.

"Emigration of the Huguenots" by Jan Neuhuys

As mentioned before in this book, the Huguenots were a French Protestant denomination that is virtually extinct due to persecution. It is quite likely that the vast majority of your ancestors came from families that were members of this group before they abjured and became Catholics – sometimes under threat of death. This realization only came after visiting the Huguenot Museum in La Rochelle.

By going to France, you get a sense for what your ancestors left behind, what the land was like, what the environment was like, why they left, and what was important to them. By going to Quebec you get a sense for what they left for, the hardships they faced, and what they had to survive. This will enrich your understanding of your forefathers and foremothers and make you a better genealogist.

If you do go to France, the city of La Rochelle is a must. When New France was lost to the British in 1759 the economy of this beautiful city died, so the downtown is essentially as it was back in the 18th and 17th century. Explore the surrounding area, including nearby cities such as Saint Jean D'Angely, Rochefort and Saintes, because they also produced many of your ancestors. Visit the Charente Maritime archives in La Rochelle not so much for their records, but for the books that they have.

Places to visit that are closer to home: New Orleans in the old French territory of Louisiana,

Acadia in what are now the Maritime Provinces of Canada, and Montreal in what was once called New France. However, the place you *must* visit is Old Quebec. When you go there you are stepping back in time - just as you will when you visit La Rochelle.

Places for Your "Bucket List"

If you have a "bucket list" – places you want to see in your lifetime – be sure to add some of the fascinating places you are sure to come across as you research your forebearers. For me one of those places was the stone home of the first of my line to be born in the New World. He built this house in the year 1700. Another special place was the church that my 10th Great Grandparents were married in back in the year 1629. I had the privilege of standing in the spot where they said "I do" almost four hundred years later. Another bucket list spot was visiting the last home that my ancestors occupied in the old country. They left it in 1905, and I visited a little over a hundred years later. The next section after this one relates the strange experience I had there.

"We carry a new world here, in our hearts. That world is growing this minute."

\- Buenaventura Durruti

Ancestral Adventures

Adventure awaits those who move beyond the confines of home and computer, and venture out on a trip to see where your kin originated.

If you travel to your ancestral homeland, you will experience adventures that are not possible if you spend all of your days on a computer in the comfort of your home looking at old records.

Among the places I recommend that you visit in France are the Huguenot museum, the Charente Maritime Archives, as well as the old city of La Rochelle. In Canada, I suggest you visit the archives in Montreal, as well as the city of old Quebec. In the United States, you may want to visit the Family History Library in Salt Lake City where a huge collection of books related to genealogy awaits you.

To date, the story that follows is what I consider the most intriguing of my genealogical journeys.

The Séance

"Que fais tu ici?" the lady asked. She was short, her gray hair arranged in a bun, and her long flowery dress had no sleeves. She had just caught me snooping around her little farm house on this hot August day in Southern France. Goats roamed the pasture next to it.

I asked her in my limited French if she spoke English, to which she replied "Non." I was in a part of the country where they have very few tourists, and I suddenly wished that I had been a better student in French class. However, my phone had a translation app, so I had her repeat her question into it. "What are you doing here?" was what the lady had asked.

"My ancestors lived in your house," I said into my device. Then I listened as it translated my words into her language.

We were standing outside her cute little maison, on a farm near St Jean D'Angely. It was a long and narrow two story home, with green shutters, crème colored walls with a hint of yellow, and a red tile roof. The tile was the same as I had back on the roof of my home back in the desert of California, which told me that this area was no stranger to heat. I noticed a tiny lizard scurry up one of the two large baby blue planters that guarded her front door, each with a large Ficus bush. An assortment of potted plants dotted the compound, but it was by no means messy. The farm upon which the house stood was immaculate. I could see a few goats in the adjacent pasture.

I had attracted her attention by peeking through the iron gates that led into the courtyard of her home, taking photographs, when she finally decided to engage me from the other side of the metal bars.

"I am Lawrence. My ancestors used to live here," I repeated into my translator, not sure if it was accurate and hoping that it didn't misinterpret and produce something offensive or ridiculous. This time she slowly nodded *yes*, confirming that she understood. I continued, "My great grandmother died in this house."

At this revelation, she became excited and talked directly into the translator. "My name is Helene. I am a medium. I can speak to the dead."

I was intrigued, but not because of my long dead ancestor. I thought of the son I had lost to cancer just two years earlier. The lady asked me if I would like to attend a séance. Pushing aside my skepticism, I accepted her invitation. "Demain" she said. *Tomorrow.*

It did not matter to me whether she could communicate with the departed or not - I had just been invited inside the last house my ancestors had occupied in Europe. I thought of the photo opportunities I would get. But in the back of my mind skepticism was giving way to hope - I wanted to talk to my son.

We chatted for a little while longer and concluded our discussion by making an appointment for 4pm tomorrow. Sometimes in America we say "arrivederci". This is what I said to her, and she understood the Italian way of saying good bye. This made her smile.

Only later did I think that it was strange to be invited into a stranger's house for a séance. Was I going to find myself in a room with a levitating table, or in a boiling pot surrounded by onions, carrots, and seasoning? The "Lawrence for dinner" thoughts were dispelled by Marguerite, the innkeeper at the hotel I was staying at. She knew this lady and vouched for her. "We get all of the cheese for our restaurant from them," Marguerite had told me in excellent English, "They have the best goat cheese."

The next day I went back to the farmhouse. Standing on the other side of the gate, I pushed the intercom button. "Bonjour Helene. Laurent ici." *Hello Helen, Lawrence here.*

An electric motor whirred as the gate slid open allowing me to pass into the court yard. She met me at the door and invited me in. I used the translator to say "Marguerite from the hotel says hello." She smiled and said something I did not understand, but I nodded as if I did. She motioned me to sit at the kitchen table. As I looked around the kitchen I noticed the thick open beams of the ceiling, hundreds of years old. Then I felt the warmth produced by the knick knacks on her shelves and the family heirlooms that surrounded me. I could almost see my own ancestors in this room.

My imagination took me to my great-grand mother, dying of a disease while only in her early 30's, the medicine men of her day unable to stop the tuberculosis that was killing her. She was surrounded by her children, one of whom would continue a line that would extend all the way to the present, to me. Now I was standing here in her house, deep in the heart of southwest France, with a person who claimed to be able to communicate with the dead.

"Asseyez-vous," she said. *Sit down.*

"Avec qui souhaitez-vous parler?" *With whom do you wish to speak?*

I thought of my son, but did not mention him. She looked at me for a moment longer before I spoke. "My great grandmother's name was Madeleine Lemay. She's the one who died in this house." In truth several "great, great, greats" needed to be added to the word grandmother to be accurate. My machine translated.

A small violet box sat on the table and she lifted the lid off. From it she pulled out a chain with a pendulum in the shape of an elongated heart at the end of it. Both were made of gold. She held the end of the chain high and let the pendulum swing about four inches above the surface of the dark wooden table. Then she said in French "Once I make contact with your grandmother she will answer through this pendulum. Clockwise means her answer is yes, counter means no. Do you understand?" Helene's eyes were closed and her face tight as she focused. She let the jewelry dangle for a minute and then said "She's here. What would you like to ask her?"

"Did you die in an accident?" Counter clockwise movement. *No.*

"Did you die from an illness?" *Yes.*

"Was it cancer?" *No.* "Was it tuberculosis?" *Yes.*

I looked up toward the open beams of the ceiling and said "Thank you Grandma Madeleine. We still remember you down here on Earth." Then my gaze shifted back to my medium whose eyes were still closed. "I would like to talk to someone else," I said to Helene through my translation program.

The pendulum swung, back and forth. Neither clockwise nor counter, just from side to side. A minute went by when she finally said in French, "He's here. Ask your questions."

"Are you my grandfather?" The pendulum swung in a counterclockwise movement - *No.* "My Dad?" *No.* "Is this Wyatt?" I asked mentioning my son's name. The pendulum swung clockwise. *Yes.*

"Have you seen grandpa?" Clockwise. *Yes.*

"Are you happy?" The pendulum stopped moving. Almost like an invisible hand had reached out and grabbed it.

"Are you in a good place?" Clockwise.

"Do you miss someone?" Clockwise.

"Me?" Counter clockwise. I'm glad he's not missing me, sort of.

I looked at the medium for a half a minute before asking, "Emily?" The pendulum began a rapid clockwise rotation. By the time he had died at 22 years old, he had been with Emily for six years. They were completely in love.

*****

After the séance, I left Helene's house still thinking about my son. I also had some great pictures of my ancestor's home.

"It's time to say goodbye, but I think goodbyes are sad and I'd much rather say hello. Hello to a new adventure."

- Ernie Harwell

Conclusion

Be thankful that you are French Canadian, because your genealogical record is one of the most complete in the world. Much of your pedigree has already been well researched; you just have to compile it. Appreciate that your 17th century ancestors colonized a world that was completely alien to them in an effort to give their children, and their children's children, a better life.

Thanks for reading my book. If you enjoyed it, please rate and review "French Canadian Roots" on websites or in literary publications.

- Lawrence Compagna

Glossary of Terms

Acadia – was a colony of New France in northeastern North America that included parts of eastern Quebec, the Maritime Provinces, and Maine from 1604 until 1713.

Acadian expulsion – the forced removal by the British of the Franco-Acadian people from the present day Canadian Maritime provinces of Nova Scotia, New Brunswick, and Prince Edward Island from 1755 to 1764. The expulsion occurred during the French and Indian War and was part of the British military campaign against New France. The British first deported Acadians to the Thirteen Colonies, and after 1758, transported additional Acadians to Britain and France. In all, approximately 11,500 out of 14,000 total Acadians were deported.

Abjure - solemnly renounce (a belief, cause, or claim). For example, the Huguenot Protestants were forced to abjure and accept the Catholic faith.

Ahnentafel - is a genealogical numbering system for listing a person's direct ancestors in a fixed sequence of ascent. It has been used since 1590.

Ancestry - one's family or ethnic descent.

Angevin Empire - the possessions of the Angevin kings of England, who also held extensive lands in France during the 12th and 13th centuries, most notably Aquitaine and Normandy.

Antiquity - the ancient past, especially the period before the Middle Ages.

Aquitaine - a traditional region of France situated in the south-western part of the country, along the Atlantic Ocean and the Pyrenees mountain range on the border with Spain. In Medieval times it was a duchy and a kingdom.

Archives - a collection of historical documents or records providing information about a place, institution, or group of people.

Assembly – putting together the work of other genealogists to form a pedigree.

Battle of Hastings - was fought in England in 1066 between the Norman-French army of William, the Duke of Normandy, and an English army under the Anglo-Saxon King Harold Godwinson. The decisive Norman victory gave

William and his descendants the throne of England.

Battle of the Plains of Abraham - was a pivotal battle in the Seven Years' War (referred to as the French and Indian War to describe the North American theatre). The battle, which began on September 13th 1759, was fought on a plateau by the British Army and Navy against the French Army, just outside the walls of Quebec City. It marks the end of French colonial power in North America. By 1763, most French possessions on the continent were ceded to the British.

Cajun - Former residents and their descendants of Acadia (see "Acadia" in this glossary). They are known as Acadians, and later as Cajuns, the English (mis)pronunciation of 'Cadiens, after resettlement in Louisiana.

Charlemagne – was a Franco-German monarch who lived between 742 and 814. After uniting much of western and central Europe during the Early Middle Ages, he was the recognized as the first Holy Roman Emperor in the year 800.

Colonist - a settler in or inhabitant of a colony such as New France, Louisiana, Acadia or the New England colonies.

Commune – A commune is the smallest French territorial division for administrative purposes.

Database - a structured set of data held in a computer, especially one that is accessible in various ways.

Decennial - recurring every ten years, as in "decennial tables" that are an index of records found in a French commune organized by decade.

Department – France is organized by department, similar to the way the United States is organized into states and Canada into provinces.

Descendent – is a person who can trace their lineage from an individual.

Descent from Antiquity (DFA) is the project of establishing a well-researched, generation-by-generation descent of living persons from people living in antiquity. It is an ultimate challenge in prosopography and genealogy.

Diaspora - the dispersion of any people from their original homeland.

Direct ancestor – someone who is in the direct line of your pedigree. They are an "x times" grandfather or "x times" grandmother.

DNA – is an acronym for deoxyribonucleic acid, a self-replicating material which is present in nearly all living organisms as the main constituent of chromosomes. It is the carrier of genetic information.

Ethnicity - the fact or state of belonging to a social group that has a common national or cultural tradition.

Family tree – refer to "pedigree".

Feudalism - the dominant social system in medieval Europe, in which the nobility held lands from the Crown in exchange for military service, and vassals were in turn tenants of the nobles, while the peasants (villeins or serfs) were obliged to live on their lord's land and give him homage, labor, and a share of the produce, notionally in exchange for military protection.

GEDCOM – abbreviation for "Genealogical Data Communication", which is a file format developed by the Church of Jesus Christ of Latter-Day Saints (LDS) as a means to facilitate the exchange of genealogical data between different genealogy programs.

Genealogy - the study and tracing of lines of descent, or a line of descent traced continuously from an ancestor.

Generation - a set of members of a family regarded as a single step or stage in descent.

Huguenot - a French Protestant of the 16th–17th centuries. Largely Calvinist, the Huguenots suffered severe persecution at the hands of the Catholic majority, and many thousands emigrated from France.

Indenture – means to bind (someone) by an indenture as an apprentice or laborer. The contract is a form of forced servitude common in the North American colonies but which is now outlawed as a form of slavery.

"Kings Daughters" - is a term used to refer to the approximately 800 young French women who immigrated to New France between 1663 and 1673 as part of a program sponsored by King Louis XIV of France. The program was designed to boost New France's population both by encouraging male immigrants to settle there, and by promoting marriage, family formation and the birth of children. These women had to have a Catholic priest vouch for their moral character to qualify. They were usually the offspring of good families where the father had died. The King himself provided their marriage dowry.

LDS – abbreviation for "The Church of Jesus Christ of Latter-day Saints", also known as the Mormons. They maintain the world's largest library dedicated to genealogical research (The Family History Library in Salt Lake City, Utah).

Lineage - lineal descent from an ancestor; ancestry or pedigree.

Louisiana (colonial) - was an administrative district of New France. Under French control from 1682 to 1762 and 1802 to 1803, the area was named in honor of King Louis XIV, by the French explorer René-Robert Cavelier, Sieur de la Salle. It originally covered an expansive territory that included most of the drainage basin of the Mississippi River and stretched from the Great Lakes to the Gulf of Mexico and from the Appalachian Mountains to the Rocky Mountains.

Medieval - relating to the Middle Ages, lasting from the 5th to 15th centuries.

Middle Ages – the period lasting from the fall of Rome in the 5th century to the fall of Constantinople in 1453.

Migrant - a person who moves from one place to another, especially in order to find work or better living conditions.

New France - the area colonized by France in North America during a period beginning with the exploration of the Gulf of Saint Lawrence by Jacques Cartier in 1534 and ending with the cession of New France to Great Britain and Spain in 1763 under the Treaty of Paris. At its peak in 1712, it extended from Newfoundland to the Canadian prairies and from Hudson Bay to the Gulf of Mexico, including all the Great Lakes of North America.

New World - one of the names used for the majority of Earth's Western Hemisphere, specifically the Americas.

Nobility - the group of people belonging to the noble class in a kingdom, especially those with a hereditary or honorary title.

French Canadian Roots

Normandy – a region of France located in the northwestern part of the country. In medieval times it was a duchy in the Kingdom of France.

Pedigree - the recorded ancestry of a person or family.

Pioneer - a person who is among the first to explore or settle a new country or area, like the United States and Canada.

PRDH – An acronym for "The Research Program in Historical Demography", which is a project of the University of Montreal. In the context of this book, it refers to the database they maintain as part of that project.

Primary Research – is the action of studying old documents and books to learn details about ancestors in order to put together a family tree.

Primogeniture - the right of succession belonging to the firstborn child, especially the feudal rule by which the whole real estate of an intestate passed to the eldest son.

Progeny - a descendant or the descendants of a person.

"Reign of Terror" - a period of remorseless repression or bloodshed associated with the French Revolution in the late 18th century.

Removed – separated by a particular number of steps of descent or by generation, as in "second cousin once removed".

Rootsweb – A website containing many GEDCOM files which in turn contain thousands of ancestors. (See "GEDCOM"). As of the time of writing the site was under construction. In the past it had been one of the foremost places to share information with other genealogists on North American genealogy.

Royal Gateway Ancestor – A forefather or foremother who is from the noble class and can therefore trace their pedigree for many generations, sometimes back into the Middle Ages and to Holy Roman Emperor Charlemagne who lived in the 8th - 9th centuries.

Saint Lawrence River French settlers – refers to the colonists of New France, the first Europeans to populate the Saint Lawrence River area of Canada and the United States in the 17th century.

William the Conqueror – the first Franco-Norman King of England beginning in 1066. See "Battle of Hastings".

About the Author

Lawrence Compagna is a Canadian-American genealogist. He was born on a brisk winter day in Cold Lake, Canada to French Canadian parents. It was on a Friday the 13th. Ignoring superstition he chooses to live his life as if it is lucky, traveling the world with pen in hand. He is an author, management consultant, genealogist, and father of three who now lives in Southern California.

Made in United States
North Haven, CT
11 December 2023

45518853R00129